D0070496

THE WAR AT HOME

for Susan and George
with good wishes
Frances Fox Piven

THE WAR AT HOME

The Domestic Costs
of Bush's Militarism

FRANCES FOX PIVEN

THE NEW PRESS

NEW YORK
LONDON

© 2004 by Frances Fox Piven
All rights reserved.
No part of this book may be reproduced, in any form, without written
permission from the publisher.

Requests for permission to reproduce selections from this book
should be mailed to: Permissions Department, The New Press, 38 Greene Street,
New York, NY 10013

Published in the United States by The New Press, New York, 2004
Distributed by W. W. Norton & Company, Inc., New York

LIBRARY OF CONGRESS CATALOGING-IN-PUBLICATION DATA

Piven, Frances Fox.
The war at home : the domestic causes and consequences of Bush's militarism /
Frances Fox Piven.
p. cm.
Includes bibliographical references.
ISBN 1-56584-935-3 (hc.)
1. United States.—Politics and government—2001- 2. Militarism—United
States. 3. Bush, George W. (George Walker), 1946- 4. War on Terrorism, 2001-
5. Terrorism—Government policy—United States. I. Title.

E902.P57 2004
973.931—dc22
2004049866

The New Press was established in 1990 as a not-for-profit alternative to the large,
commercial publishing houses currently dominating the book publishing
industry. The New Press operates in the public interest rather than for private
gain, and is committed to publishing, in innovative ways, works of educational,
cultural, and community value that are often deemed insufficiently profitable.

www.thenewpress.com

Composition by Westchester Composition
Copyediting by icopyedit

Printed in the United States of America

2 4 6 8 10 9 7 5 3 1

CONTENTS

ACKNOWLEDGMENTS

I WANT TO thank the friends who gave me advice, passed me bits of information, and shared their good spirits, including Barbara Ehrenreich, Lori Minnite, Magali Larson, Dorothea Benz, Peter Gowan, Penny Lewis, and Brian Waddell. I also want to thank my excellent editor, Andy Hsiao, and my agent and dear friend Frances Goldin.

THE WAR AT HOME

THE WAR AT HOME

THIS BOOK EXAMINES the domestic political dynamics that accompanied America's unilateral turn toward preemptive war.

A great deal has been said about the American goals for the wars in Afghanistan and Iraq, much of it summed up by the term "imperialism." Much also has been said about the international consequences of these wars. I agree that the United States is an imperial power, and that the international consequences of our new aggressions—the loss of American standing in the world, our eroded alliances, the spread of terrorism—are all-important. However, a singular fixation on the international dimensions of U.S. policy is turning our eyes away from the under-examined domestic politics of the "new" imperialism. It is also turning us away from the potential for domestic resistance to this new phase of imperialism, resistance that may be capable of curbing our military aggression.

In the pages that follow, I present three arguments. First, war overseas always has a home front—and domestic fallout. The current wars were promoted—and fed—by the powerful U.S. military establishment and the inner networks of neo-conservative intellectuals and think tanks linked to the military establishment. These wars also, at least temporarily, helped resolve political tensions between the right wing think tanks, faith-based interest groups, and other factions on the right that surround and penetrate the current federal regime. Moreover, and enormously important, from the initial announcement of a war on terror in the wake of 9/11 to the continuing occupation of Iraq, U.S. military aggression has served to shore up voter support for the Bush administration. The rush of patriotism and jingoism that inevitably follow in the wake of war was surely anticipated, along with the electoral advantage this gave to the Republican Party and to a president who took office under the cloud of a disputed election and whose popular support was falling in the polls.

Second, the emotional fervor generated by these wars smoothed the way for huge advances in the domestic neoconservative agenda. The business interests backing that agenda, with its emphasis on social spending cuts, regulation rollbacks, and regressive restructuring of the tax system, have been influential in American politics for several decades, and especially since the 1980 election. But they have always been resisted, so that progress has been slower than conservatives would prefer. There are huge and predatory profits at stake here. Consider only the long-term right-wing campaign to privatize Social Security and Medicare, the base programs of the American welfare state. These programs are popular — Social Security is often referred to as the "third rail" of American politics — and the effort to discredit them to pave the way for privatization has been stubbornly resisted, both by the public and by Congress. The president's poll ratings were low and falling before their post-9/11 boost, and then declined again until the invasion of Iraq.

The war on terror and then the war on Iraq each gave Bush a lift in the polls, generating the support for the commander in chief and his party that made new inroads on these and other social programs possible.[1] When House Speaker Dennis Hastert worried, for example, that some Republicans would defect on a vote to defeat the Corporate Patriot Enforcement Act (intended to crack down on offshore corporate tax dodges), he called on them not to embarrass the president in a time of war.[2] And remember Tom DeLay's belligerent assertion during the congressional debate over the second of Bush's huge tax cuts that "nothing is more important in the face of war than cutting taxes," no matter that the tax cuts devoured the Social Security surplus.[3] A moment's thought reveals the statement as ludicrous, which brings me to my third point.

The conduct of America's current wars violates the lessons of history. Historically, governments waging war sooner or later tried to compensate their people for the blood and wealth they sacrificed. As war continued and the rush of patriotic fervor faded, governments tried to shore up support by expanding democratic rights, making the rich share some of the costs through increased taxation, and initiating or expanding social welfare programs.

This period is markedly different. During World War II, tax rates on the rich rose to 90 percent; during our current wars, taxes on the rich have been slashed. Toward the end of World War I, the franchise was expanded in war-weary Britain, Woodrow Wilson announced his support for collective bargaining, and toward the end of the Vietnam War, eighteen-year-olds were given the right to vote in the United States; our current wars have so far seen the stripping away of civil liberties and a sustained assault on unions. And at the end of World War II, European nations vastly expanded their health, housing, and income security programs, and the United States initiated a remarkably generous veterans' benefit program. During the current period, social welfare programs are being cut, both at the federal and the state level, and even some veterans' benefits have been reduced.

This pattern suggests a developing regime vulnerability. My concluding pages will examine the potential for domestic resistance generated by the home front in America's imperial wars.

*   *   *

Attacks on American troops continue in Iraq. More than 750 are dead, several thousand injured, and untold more exposed to the long-term aftereffects of munitions that use depleted uranium casings. At the end of March 2004, after an American convoy hit a bomb planted in a street in Falluja, four "security consultants" were shot, their bodies torn apart and dragged through the streets by a jeering mob,[4] setting off a string of reactions sparking Shiite and Sunni uprisings throughout the country. Iraqis who collaborate with the occupation administration are increasingly the victims of guerilla attacks, including not only the new inductees to the Iraqi police force, but reportedly also professionals and politicians working with the American authorities. The death toll of Iraqi civilians has reached about 10,000. Well-armed Kurdish, Sunni, and Shiite militias are resisting American pressure to disband. Infrastructure remains weak, and widespread looting continues.

In early March 2004, suicide bombings in Baghdad and Karbala killed at least 200 Shiite pilgrims on the Muslim holiday Ashura, evoking prospects of the revival of centuries-old Sunni violence against Shiites that could spread across the Middle East and South Asia. "It is virtually unthinkable," said Vali Nasr in the *New York Times,* "to many Sunnis that one of the most important Arab countries—the seat of the Abbasid Empire from the eighth to thirteenth centuries, which established Sunni supremacy and brutally suppressed Shiites—would pass from Sunni to Shiite domination. In militant Sunni circles, it is taken as proof of an American conspiracy against them and against Islam as a whole."[5] Meanwhile, Afghanistan may be headed for a return to a regime of warlords and opium, of Taliban domination and chaos, and the possibility looms of new assertions of U.S. military power in that region.

American military aggression in the post–World War II period is of course not new.[6] What is new is the public bravado and doggedness with which the current wars were pursued in the face of worldwide opposition. But, though great rivers of words have poured forth, the reasons for this new sort of unilateral war and the in-your-face posture with which it was undertaken and is now defended, remain murky.

There are official explanations, of course, but they slip about, fastening on one rationale until discrediting evidence emerges, and then turning to another until it too falls under the weight of evidence. In fact, Bush campaigned in the 2000 election with rhetoric that disdained foreign entanglements and especially "nation building." We have since learned, however, that key groups in the new administration came to office with ambitions to curb "rogue states" and to assert American military power across the globe, especially in the oil-rich Middle East. Iraq, with its large oil reserves, and weakened by a decade of misgovernment and sanctions, was the place they wanted to begin. We can also surmise from the plans unveiled by the Pentagon once the invasion was over and the occupation had begun, that Iraq is to be one of the "forward operating sites" in a planned expansion of American military capacity worldwide.[7]

The public arguments, however, emphasized the danger Iraq's weapons of mass destruction posed to the United States. A series of authoritative analyses now make it clear that Iraq did not harbor weapons of mass destruction. Not only did flawed American intelligence reports vastly overstate the threat, these reports were then further exaggerated by the Bush administration.[8] And rather than making the United States and the world safer, the war in Iraq has spurred Iran's nuclear ambitions, while North Korea appears to have embarked on a program to produce hundreds of warheads in the next decade. Our designation of Pakistan as a "major non-NATO ally" stands despite revelations of its active exchange of nuclear and missile technology with North Korea.[9] The federal government has quietly acknowledged the increased threats by reviving a program to study nuclear fallout.[10]

Nor has any evidence surfaced to support the administration's unlikely claim that secular Iraq was linked to the fiercely religious al-Qaeda, another justification for war. The wars in Afghanistan and Iraq in fact increased the terrorist threat. As Chalmers Johnson points out, while there were five major al-Qaeda attacks worldwide between 1993 and 9/11, there were seventeen such attacks in the next two years.[11] The evidence points to al-Qaeda in the bombing of commuter trains in Madrid in March 2004, the deadliest terror attack in Europe since World War II. The attack left hundreds dead, brought millions of Spaniards into the streets, and resulted in the defeat of the government that had collaborated with the United States.[12]

Finally, there is the familiar "regime change" explanation: once Saddam Hussein was toppled, Iraq would emerge as a model democracy in the Arab world, encouraging democratic currents elsewhere in the Middle East, or at least intimidating totalitarian rulers. The "most idealistic war in modern times," wrote David Ignatius, the *Washington Post* commentator.[13] Instead, American aggression has fueled fundamentalism and sparked new terrorist assaults in Saudi Arabia, Morocco, and Indonesia.

Of course, the administration's claims are propaganda intended to justify war-making, and no thoughtful observer would expect the leaders of a state at war to do less than justify their own actions. But the explanations of academic critics for these new wars are not entirely satisfactory either. There are the straightforward geopolitical arguments that explain American aggression in Iraq as a grab for its rich oil resources,[14] or the war in Afghanistan as an effort to gain military bases not only in Afghanistan but also in Azerbaijan, Georgia, and Turkey, which would ensure control of a prospective multibillion dollar pipeline to carry Caspian oil to the West.[15] In February 2004 a consortium of international oil companies formally agreed to proceed with a $29 billion development of the large Kashagan oil field in Kazakhstan.[16] Or, as Kevin Phillips suggests, domination of Iraq is intended by our leaders to shore up American domination in the region by replacing the increasingly unreliable Saudis, whose oil reserves may in any case be declining, with a totally reliable Iraq.[17] To those who argue the United States did not need more oil, there are less direct variants of the geopolitical explanation that see preemptive war not as a means of grabbing oil in the short run but rather for the longer run when available supplies run short,[18] or less directly still, as a strategy of asserting domination over Europe and China by controlling the main oil resources of the world.[19]

Or there are systemic arguments that locate the motor for our new foreign wars in crises arising from the dynamics of American capitalism. Immanuel Wallerstein thinks the United States needed to go to war in Iraq to demonstrate America's overwhelming military power, a demonstration that would intimidate European nations freed from their dependence on the United States by the demise of the Soviet threat, and also intimidate third world powers pursuing nuclear armaments.[20] Peter Gowan similarly argues the importance of displaying America's military prowess to shore up "global hegemony" and to foil emerging European efforts to achieve autonomy.[21] David Harvey sees the new imperialism as driven by the internal contradictions of capital accumulation, and specifically the need to find outlets for surplus capital.[22] And Chalmers Johnson also sees the United States as "a military juggernaut intent on world domination."[23] Elsewhere Johnson says, "establishing a more impressive footprint has now become part of the new justification for a major enlargement of our empire. . . with a preventive war strategy against 'rogue states,' 'bad guys,' and 'evil-doers'" across an "arc of instability" running through the third world.[24] Others argue that military assertion was driven by the need to protect a weak U.S. economy, suffering from bloated trade and budget deficits and a plummeting dollar, from the danger of foreign disinvestment.[25]

There is no disputing that the United States is the dominant military power in the world and that it uses its power to extract resources from elsewhere, especially from the southern hemisphere, and to force economic policies on nations that favor American capital. These are the classic motives of imperial powers. Before the current wars, the United States was already the dominant imperial power in the world. American corporations extracted other nations' resources on favorable terms, and the American state wielded strong influence over the policies of most nations. "[T]he entire advanced-capitalist zone was integrated without much strain into an informal American imperium, whose landmarks were Bretton Woods, the Marshall and Dodge Plans, NATO and U.S.–Japan Security Pact," writes Perry Andersen.[26]

Military power was important in this domination. But the use of overt force was restrained, exercised mainly in the immediate sphere of American influence in the western hemisphere (Grenada, Panama), or through covert military actions (Chile), as well as through assassinations and coups. These forms of military intervention did not command the world's attention because they were undertaken by the CIA or by client regimes. There were also military actions undertaken in cooperation with other powers, or under the aegis of NATO or the UN, which could be presented to the world as multilateral policing actions. In the 1990s, the

United States intervened in this way in Bosnia, East Timor, Haiti, Kosovo, and Somalia, and deployed a kind of gunboat diplomacy against Afghanistan, China, North Korea, Sudan, and of course Iraq.[27]

The strategy of multilateralism in turn lent American domination a considerable degree of legitimacy, a legitimacy enhanced by the worldwide spread of American popular culture. "For America is part of everyone's imaginative life," writes Timothy Garton Ash, "through movies, music, television and the Web, whether you grow up in Bilbao, Beijing, or Bombay. Everyone has a New York in their heads, even if they have never been there—which is why the destruction of the twin towers had such an impact."[28] Joseph Nye calls this American "soft power," the power to persuade that greatly augments military power by making its exercise less necessary.[29] Multilateralism thus magnified American power (which Ivo Daalder and James Lindsay say the Bush regime simply didn't understand).[30]

So, why the radical shift? U.S. military might was clearly overwhelming and undisputed. Why was a costly new demonstration necessary? Were there looming threats to the imperium, to "existing patterns of ownership, investment, trade, or access to resources" as in Arundhati Roy's formulation?[31] What strategic calculus demonstrated this display of military capacity was worth its probable costs in frayed multilateral ties and in the worldwide loss of American legitimacy?

Many intellectuals, both on the left and the right, think the current wars make little sense. Indeed, they judge current U.S. policy to be totally reckless, if not lunatic. "Looking back over the forty years of the Cold War," writes Arthur M. Schlesinger Jr., "we can be everlastingly grateful that the loonies on both sides were powerless. In 2003, however, they run the Pentagon, and preventive war—the Bush doctrine—is now official policy." Eric Hobsbawm sums up the view: "The sudden emergence of an extraordinary, ruthless, antagonistic flaunting of U.S. power is hard to understand, all the more so since it fits neither with long-tested imperial policies developed during the Cold War, nor the interests of the U.S. economy. The policies that have recently prevailed in Washington seem to all outsiders so mad that it is difficult to understand what is really intended." Hobsbawm goes on to assert the "frivolity of U.S. decision making"; by weakening all the international arrangements for keeping order, formal and informal, there is the danger of "destabilizing of the world."[32]

Mainstream leaders in the foreign policy establishment agree. Even the hawkish Zbigniew Brzezinski, President Carter's national security advisor, told a Washington D.C. symposium in October that "American power worldwide is at its historic nadir" because of its paranoiac view of the world, because its fear of terrorism verges on panic, and is stoked by "extreme demagogy." Serge Schmemann of the *International Herald Tribune* says the new American order "has generated a tsunami of anti-Americanism, with the United States perceived in some quarters as a greater threat than al-Qaeda."[33] Even Margaret Tutweiler, the new State Department official in charge of public diplomacy, acknowledges "it will take us many years of hard, focused work" to restore America's standing in the world.[34] From the perspective of those in the more Wilsonian foreign policy establishment who believe that America's foreign policy goals should be pursued through multilateral alliances and institutions, and shrouded in claims of promoting peace, democracy, and markets, the militarism and unilateralism of the war on Iraq is ominous.[35] "A great philosophical schism has opened with the West," writes Robert Kagan and . . . mutual antagonism threatens to debilitate both sides of the transatlantic community."[36]

There is even dissent from the military. The Army War College issued a report in January 2004 calling the war in Iraq "unnecessary" and the war on terror "unrealistic."[37] And Brian Urquhart sums up his catalog of the "strange and unsettling developments of the first four years of the twenty-first century with "the opening of a dangerous gulf of misunderstanding between the United States and much of the rest of the world; the growing, and terrifying, threat of nuclear proliferation; and the proclamation by the United States of the policy of preventive and preemptive war and at least one questionable experiment with it. The relative optimism that attended the beginning of the century has largely evaporated."[38] Not only had the United States declared its right to undertake preemptive war, but it had pulled out of the major multilateral initiatives to deal with international problems, including the Kyoto Protocol to check global warming and the International Criminal Court; it had sabotaged an effort to give muscle to the biological weapons convention; it denigrated the Security Council; and dismissed NATO allies as "old Europe."[39]

So, the puzzle remains. Why the turn to preemptive war and, relatedly, the cavalier treatment of the painstakingly constructed multilateral arrangements of the past half century? I don't think the question can be fully answered if the war in Iraq is regarded solely as a foreign policy strategy. The war is also a domestic strategy, rooted not only in calculations of America's global power, but in calculations geared to shoring up the Bush regime's domestic power and its ability to pursue its domestic policy agenda. To suggest a domestic dimension of foreign policy is actually not particularly novel. That the Cold War was useful because it justified the domestic Red Scare of the 1950s and the resultant taming of American labor is a common enough observation, for example. Margaret Thatcher went to war in the Falkland Islands not to restore British imperial power but for the boost it gave her among an enthusiastic British electorate.

A number of analysts have pointed more generally to the domestic functions of external aggression, as when David Harvey, after citing Hannah Arendt's observation that state authority requires "external props," refers, however briefly, to the "relation between the internal and external conditions of political power." In his reading, 9/11 provided the political opening to name an evil external enemy that allowed the regime to "proclaim national solidarity, [and] also to impose order and stability on civil society at home."[40] But Harvey's main analytic interest is in the ways that foreign war serves contemporary American capitalism, not only by providing a "spatial fix" for a crisis-prone system of capital accumulation, but ultimately by making possible "accumulation by dispossession." In other words, military aggression is a strategy of plunder. I don't disagree. But I think in this case, military aggression also paved the political way for policies that are plundering Americans. The predatory beast was turning on its own. I turn first to the ways that war shored up the regime's power at home.

THE WAR AS A POWER STRATEGY

EXPLANATIONS FOCUSING ON imperialism assume the main reason for war in Iraq was to shore up American domination abroad. I argue that another reason for war was to shore up America's rulers at home. War-making satisfied powerful domestic interest groups who were pushing for a military buildup. The fear and excitement generated by war helped paper over fissures in the Republican base. And the war figured importantly in the electoral strategy of the president and his party. As I will show in the next chapter, with the political lift gained by war-making, the Bush regime was also able to push rapidly ahead with its right wing domestic policy agenda. The agenda was predatory, not in the imperial sense of extracting wealth from foreign peoples, but in the more pedestrian sense of extracting wealth from the American people. This is not to dismiss the family of analyses that see preemptive war as a strategy for imperial domination. It is reasonable to think the governing regime of a large and complex country is subject to multiple and complex pressures. Nevertheless, attention to domestic politics helps explain a course of action that otherwise seems less than fully rational.

THE MILITARY INDUSTRIAL ESTABLISHMENT

First, war answers the demands of claimants in the Bush inner circle. Very important among those claimants is the huge American military establishment which includes the armed forces, the intelligence agencies, defense contractors, and the research institutions and think tanks to which they are linked. Some of the neo-con intellectuals usually fingered as the main warmongers are associated with this establishment, while others derive much of their influence from the fact that they provide the ideological arguments that justify ever-increasing American military capabilities.

We usually think of the military as an institution that is built up to prosecute war. And of course the military is the instrument of American imperial designs. If this were the whole of it, then the size and power of the establishment would rise and fall with foreign war, more the consequence of international conflicts than a cause of such conflicts. For much of American history, this seems to have been more or less true. Even the enormous military expansion of World War II was followed by demobilization, both of troops and defense factories. But the Cold War that rapidly ensued spurred a new buildup of the military that was never reversed. The armed forces and the intelligence agencies grew, as did the industries that supplied them, and their far-flung allies multiplied in research institutions and universities, in think tanks, and in government. Whatever the initiating motives or the raison d'etre of this establishment, it has now become a major force in its own right, ready and able to generate the ideas and even the events that justify its stability and growth. Thus, so long as massive American forces were deployed in Europe to counter the presumed Soviet threat, the Soviet Union would in turn maintain the forces that made that threat credible.[1] And so long as the Soviet threat remained credible, the military establishment thrived. Real defense spending bobbed up and down a little, but never declined to near pre–World War II levels, averaging $281 billion a year in 2002 dollars between 1950 and 2002.[2]

Consider the staggering scale of the armed forces alone. To be sure, the numbers here have declined since the fall of the Soviet Union. Still, some 1.4 million men and women remain under arms, with a payroll of roughly $80 billion. And the armed forces ought reasonably to include the people who work for private security companies. These are effectively mercenaries operating under the radar screen of official public policy, but they are paid with government funds, and they are replacing government troops in conflicts around the world. In Colombia, for example, they conduct secret search and surveillance operations.[3] And they are increasingly important in Iraq, where the occupation has led to an explosive growth in the industry with some two dozen private military companies employing as many as 20,000 people in the field.[4] The attacks on four of these security employees in Falluja in the spring of 2004 brought the use of mercenaries to public attention, at least momentarily.

Johnson writes of an "empire of bases," meaning the roughly 1,000 or so bases that the United States owns or rents overseas, often giant establishments with quite lavish facilities.[5] But the overwhelming majority, some 6,000 military bases, are not overseas but in the United States and its territories where the bases have become integral to local economic life and a major source of profit to private companies like Halliburton, DynCorp, and the Vinnell Corporation who contract to provide base services.[6]

Then there are the sprawling intelligence agencies, with a $30 billion a year bottom line divided among fifteen agencies with a crazy-quilt division of responsibilities, most under the control of the Department of Defense, the remainder under the control of the CIA.[7] The military establishment also includes the nuclear weapons programs run by the Energy Department. The U.S. nuclear arsenal includes 5,400 multiple megaton warheads, 1,750 nuclear bombs and cruise missiles, and 1,670 tactical nuclear weapons, with an additional 10,000 nuclear weapons stored in bunkers.[8] The Star Wars lobby embraces not only the Pentagon, Lockheed Martin, and Boeing, but right-wing think tanks like the Heritage Foundation, the Center for Security Policy, and Empower America.[9] Looming in the future with the increasing use of satellite-directed missiles is the expansion of the space program recently promised by President Bush.[10] On the agenda, in other words, is the militarization of space.

The military is intimately tied to the industries that supply it, and both are closely connected to politics, especially but not solely to Republican politics. As then Secretary of War Henry L. Stimson noted in 1940, "If you are going to try to go to war, prepare for war in a capitalist country, you have to let business make money out of the process, or business won't work."[11] The Washington-based Center for Public Integrity reported that at least nine of the thirty members of the Bush administration's Defense Policy Board were connected to companies that received some $76 billion in military contracts between 2001 and 2002. Of course, this pattern of close collaboration between the military and the private corporations that supply the military did not begin with the Bush regime.

The top weapon makers such as Lockheed Martin (a merger of Martin Marietta, Loral Defense, General Dynamics, and other companies), or Boeing Northrup Grumman, which absorbed McDonnell Douglas Corp (these mergers were actually subsidized by the Pentagon under the Clinton administration), are behemoths that leave a huge political footprint that influences both parties.[12] They have hundreds of thousands of employees in factories within many congressional districts, and they are big contributors to the political parties.[13] No wonder Congress regularly adds billions to Pentagon budget requests. When Dwight D. Eisenhower left the presidency in 1961, he famously warned: "The conjunction of an immense military establishment and a large arms industry. . . . [means] the potential for the disastrous rise of misplaced power exists and will persist."[14]

The war in Iraq sparked a rush of new contracts, as U.S. multinationals were "invited to bid on everything from rebuilding roads and bridges to printing contracts," writes Naomi Klein. "Some argue that it's too simplistic to say this war is about oil," Klein comments wryly. "They're right. It's about oil, water, roads, trains, phones, ports, and drugs."[15] In the short run, at least, these contracts are being paid for not by the imperial extraction of the resources of other peoples, but by extraction from American taxpayers. The big winner in the competition to rebuild Iraq is Dick Cheney's old firm, the giant Texas oil services business Halliburton, and its subsidiary, Kellogg, Brown & Root. Halliburton received its first contract for logistical services for American troops in Iraq in 2001.[16] In September 2002, a secret task force, formed to plan for Iraq's oil industry in the event of war, granted Kellogg, Brown & Root the noncompetitive contract for up to $7 billion to rebuild Iraq's oil operations.[17] All told, Halliburton has so far received some $11 billion for its work in Iraq.[18] (Halliburton subsidiaries, incidentally, are incorporated in a variety of exotic places to avoid federal taxes).[19]

Then there is the Bechtel Group, a company that signed a $680 million contract for reconstruction in Iraq in April 2003, and received an additional $1.82 billion reconstruction contract, the first in a series, in January 2004.[20] More than seventy American companies have so far been awarded billions of dollars in Iraqi contracts, including International American Products, Perini Corporation, Contrack International, Fluor, Washington Group International, the Research Triangle Institute (with a contract for local governance), the International Resources Group (with a contract for planning and management), Stevedoring Services of America (with a contract for seaport administration), and Creative Associates International (working on primary and secondary education).[21] Not surprising, albeit hardly a stroke of diplomacy, the Pentagon has barred companies from France, Russia, Canada, and Germany from bidding on these Iraqi reconstruction contracts. It is keeping the plunder for its American corporate friends.

These companies in turn have close ties to American politicians, especially but not only to Republican politicians. Kellogg, Brown & Root began as Brown & Root, a Texas construction firm that was later acquired by Halliburton. Brown & Root was the benefactor of Lyndon Baines Johnson, and in turn profited handsomely in the Vietnam era as a space contractor, and as part of a consortium with contracts to build military projects in Vietnam.[22] When Dick Cheney was secretary of defense under the first President Bush, the Pentagon decided to turn the bulk of its military support service contracts over to a single company. Halliburton was commissioned to do a study of how this would work and was then selected as the sole company to provide support work for the next five years. In 1995, Cheney became the chief executive of Halliburton. He continues to receive $150,000 a year in deferred compensation from the firm and retains stock options worth more than $18 million.[23] To cement its political ties, Halliburton funneled more than $500,000 to the Republican Party in the last two elections, according to Common Cause.

A subsidiary of Bechtel, Bechtel National, is slated to do the work of rebuilding Iraq's roads, power plants, water systems, seaports, and airports. Bechtel's ties to the military establishment are longstanding. One of its board members, and a former president of the firm, is George Shultz, the secretary of state under Ronald Reagan, and chairman of the Committee for the Liberation of Iraq.[24] Caspar Weinberger, defense secretary under Ronald Reagan, was also associated with the firm.

The Bush family itself is tied to the military industrial complex.

Kevin Phillips has recently had much to say about the family and
its connections: "If there are other families who have more fully
epitomized and risen alongside the hundred-year emergence of
the U.S. military-industrial complex, the post-1945 national security state, and the twenty-first century imperium, no one has
identified them. Certainly no other established a presidential dynasty."[25] The dynasty's power begins with the great-grandfathers
of President Bush—George Herbert Walker and Samuel Prescott
Bush—and continues with grandfather Prescott Bush who main-
tained ties with Nazi Germany until Pearl Harbor. Elsewhere,
Phillips says that "when you get the Bushes, you get really what
amounts to a four-generation history of involvement with finance
and the oil industry . . . [and] very close ties to the intelligence
agencies of the military-industrial complex, of which the oil industry has become a major part. And obviously there are the ties
to the oil industry and the preoccupation with the Middle East
and Texas, and the price of oil."[26]

As would be true of any large network of bureaucracies, the
leaders of the military-industrial complex strive for its preserva-
tion and growth, with minimal disruption to ongoing military
and weapons systems. And they are well-positioned to accomplish
this aim. Lawrence Korb, the former assistant secretary of defense
in the Reagan administration, said when he testified before the
House Budget Committee last year: "The real reason for the increase in this year's budget is not the war against terrorism or the
state of our military. This massive increase is necessary because
the Bush administration failed to carry out its campaign promises
to transform the military and the secretary of defense failed to
make the hard choices that are necessary when formulating a defense budget. Rather, he simply layered his new programs on top
of the Clinton programs he inherited."[27]

The Pentagon finally announced plans to cancel the Comanche

helicopter program in February 2004, after twenty-one years
during which the program had not produced a single operational
aircraft. Yet, as the news of the cancellation reverberates in Con-
necticut where the helicopter is designed and built, the last word
on the fate of the Comanche may not yet have been written.[28]
Similarly, the congressional General Accounting Office report
noted "Cultural resistance to change and military service paro-
chialism have also played a significant role in impeding attempts
to implement broad-based management reforms at the Department of Defense. The department has acknowledged that it con-
fronts decades-old problems deeply grounded in the bureaucratic
history and operating practices of a complex multifaceted organization, and that many of these practices were developed piece-
meal and evolved to accommodate different organizations, each
with its own policies and procedures."[29] In the same vein, Wesley
Clark attributes the failure of the military to anticipate the debacle
in Iraq to "the military-industrial complex and the politics of
survival as an organization. . . . [T]he Army, like the other services, has made its existence dependent on high-tech innovation
and the creation of impressive, far-sighted procurement programs. . . . T]hese programs were seen as more likely to compete
for funding. And, once funded, they would get important backing
from contractors and subcontractors in many congressional districts."[30]

Chalmers Johnson describes the broad consequences of the
rise of the military-industrial establishment for American political
life. Entire regions become dependent on defense expenditures,
members of Congress work to attract defense contracts to their
districts, high-ranking military officers come to expect lavish "re-
tirement" to the defense industry, just as defense contractors in
turn receive appointments to the Pentagon. (Last year General
Tommy Franks commanded the invasion of Iraq. This year he

joined the board of Free Market Global, a company that trades in oil and gas.[31]) The result, says Johnson, is "a kind of military opportunism at the heart of government, with military men paying court to the pet schemes of inexperienced politicians and preparing for lucrative post-retirement positions in the arms industry or military think tanks."[32]

*   *   *

The growth of the military establishment is clearly not simply the consequence of foreign threats. But the military has to be able to invoke the idea of foreign threats to justify itself, and especially to justify its aggressive growth. For decades, the menace of Soviet armed power, real or contrived, provided that justification. The demise of the Soviet Union meant the loss of a rationale, spelling at least a potential problem for the future of the American military and its multiple alliances. Inevitably, a network so huge, with everything from jobs to political careers to entire communities to billions of dollars in profit hanging on it, does not find it difficult to generate the political support to guarantee its persistence. But the idea of foreign threats that make the military essential for our defense is nevertheless crucial.

This does not mean the leaders of the armed forces themselves are necessarily eager for war, except perhaps for small wars against weak antagonists. After the defeat in Vietnam, they have shown notable caution about new military expeditions that would risk their forces and their prestige, sometimes labeling the hawkish neo-cons "chicken-hawks" for their belligerence. Anthony Zinni, a retired Marine Corps general, recently scorned the ideologues who were, he said, plunging the nation into a war in a part of the world they do not understand: "The more I saw, the more I thought this was the product of the neo-cons who didn't understand the region and were going to create havoc there. These were dilettantes from Washington think tanks who never had an idea that worked on the ground."[33]

*   *   *

As Zinni indicates, the neo-cons were important. They provided the ideological rationale, and the zeal, that justified the growth of the American military. The revelations of Paul O'Neill; President Bush's former treasury secretary, make clear what many have suspected. Iraq was discussed at the very first National Security Council meeting after Bush was inaugurated and, says O'Neill, "From the beginning, there was a conviction that Saddam Hussein was a bad person and he needed to go."[34] Richard A. Clarke, counter-terrorism expert for three administrations, made the same point.[35] Investigative journalists Seymour Hersh and James Fallows also describe the pro-war conviction of a cabal within the administration.[36]

This conviction reflected the long-term influence of a closely knit group of neo-cons with long associations with both the Pentagon and right-wing think tanks, a group that Pat Buchanan not unreasonably calls the "War Party."[37] The think tank network is extensive, including the well-known American Enterprise Institute (which serves as a kind of recruitment office for the neo-cons), the Hudson Institute, the Heritage Foundation, the Free Congress Foundation, Georgetown University's Ethics and Public Policy Center, the Committee for the Free World, the Center for Security Policy, the National Institute for Public Policy, the Project for a New American Century, and the Jewish Institute for National Security. These interconnected organizations, and the journals in which the neo-cons publish, are supported by a number of conservative foundations such as Olin, the Adolph Coors

Foundation, the Smith-Richardson Foundation, and Scaife Family Trusts, as well as by midsize industrial firms, the oil industry, and the largesse of Bechtel, Lockheed Martin, the Carlyle Group, Martin Marietta, and Boeing Northrop Grumman.[38]

With the ascendance of the Bush administration, key figures from this group came to occupy important posts in the administration, particularly in the Pentagon. The network reached to Vice President Dick Cheney and the new Secretary of Defense Donald Rumsfeld.[39] It included Cheney's chief of staff, Lewis "Scooter" Libby, and Rumsfeld's deputy secretary, Paul Wolfowitz, as well as Douglas Feith, undersecretary of defense for policy. The network also included players in other Pentagon-related agencies such as the Defense Policy Board, which Richard Perle chaired until March 2003. Off-site there were other closely allied groups, such as the anti-Saddam Iraq National Congress, an exile group founded by Ahmad Chalabi, and the source of a good deal of the bogus intelligence which made its way to the highest echelons of American government. Much is sometimes made of the links that some in this network, particularly Perle and Feith, had developed with right-wing Israeli groups.[40] More important are their links with the huge American military establishment for which the War Party speaks.

The neo-cons fiercely rail against the Wilsonian multilateralism of much of the foreign policy establishment. They exalt patriotism, nationalism, and militarism as first principles, justifying, even demanding, the unilateral deployment of American military power. Their arrogance can be startling. As early as 1981, Midge Decter, a first generation neo-con, wrote: "Except in certain enclaves of absurdity and irrelevance, such as the universities and the Public Broadcasting System, virtually no one in the world believes anymore that there is a system preferable to ours: more benign, more equitable, more productive. . . . [We are] waging a 'battle of ideas.' That battle, at least among serious people is now over. We have won it."[41] As it turned out, the neo-cons did not in fact think the battle was over.

The collapse of the Soviets meant the collapse of the external threat that justified the militance of the War Party and its support for military spending and the deployment of the American military abroad. But this change seems only to have freed the War Party to widen its horizons. In 1993, Irving Kristol, another neo-con notable, announced that the demise of the Soviet Union signaled not the victory that Decter had boasted of, but a new phase in the neo-con wars: "There is no 'after the Cold War' for me. So far from having ended, my Cold War has increased in intensity, as sector after sector has been ruthlessly corrupted by the liberal ethos. Now that the other 'Cold War' is over, the real Cold War has begun. We are far less prepared for this Cold War, far more vulnerable to our enemy, than was the case with our victorious war against a global communist threat."[42]

The end of the Cold War also meant the declining importance of the post–World War II system of multilateral alliances, especially with Europe, freeing the War Party to expand its military ambitions. In 1992 a document leaked from the Pentagon office of Paul Wolfowitz called for a permanent American military presence on six continents capable of establishing and protecting a new world order. Dismissed when it was leaked to the *Washington Post* in 1992, the Wolfowitz proposal became American policy in the form of a thirty-three–page National Security Strategy memo issued by President Bush on September 21, 2002.[43] Dolores Janiewski cites a 1996 *Foreign Affairs* article by Robert Kagan and Irving Kristol that argued for a foreign policy that would assert "America's role as a global hegemon" through increased military spending and the mobilization of public opinion in support of "America's global mission" to promote democracy, free

markets, and regime change.[44] On January 26, 1998, Elliott
Abrams, Bill Bennett, Robert Kagan, William Kristol, Richard
Perle, and Paul Wolfowitz wrote to then–President Clinton begging him to use his State of the Union message to make removing
Saddam Hussein through military action the aim of American
foreign policy. And only nine days after 9/11 a longer list of neo-
cons wrote to President Bush saying that the newly declared "war
on terror" must target Hezbollah, Syria, and Iran, and overthrow
Saddam.[45]

In the wake of the conquest of Iraq, plans were afoot for a
more ambitious preventive war strategy. Chalmers Johnson reports that Andy Hoehn, deputy assistant secretary of defense for
strategy, was put in charge of drawing up a blueprint targeting
"something they call the 'arc of instability,' which is said to run
from the Andean region of South America (read: Colombia)
through North Africa and then sweeps across the Middle East to
the Philippines and Indonesia. . . . According to the American
Enterprise Institute, the idea is to create a 'global cavalry' that can
ride in from 'frontier stockades' and shoot up the 'bad guys' as
soon as we get some intelligence on them."[46]

After 9/11, the War Party's rhetoric escalated sharply. On September 12, Bill Bennett told CNN that Congress should declare
war on militant Islam with overwhelming force, citing Lebanon,
Libya, Syria, Iraq, Iran, and China as targets. The *Wall Street Journal* followed up, calling for strikes on "terrorist camps in Syria,
Sudan, Libya, and Algeria, and perhaps even parts of Egypt."[47]
Robert Jay Lifton reports that within days of 9/11, the director of
the CIA made a presentation to the president and his advisors
called "Worldwide Attack Matrix" describing active or planned
operations in eighty countries.[48] In 2003, Kristol explained the relationship between his patriotism and unilateral war: "[F]or a
great power, the 'national interest' is not a geographical term, ex-

cept for fairly prosaic matters like trade and environmental regulation. . . . And large nations, whose identity is ideological, like the
Soviet Union of yesteryear and the United States of today, inevitably have ideological interests in addition to more material
concerns. Barring extraordinary events, the United States will always feel obliged to defend, if possible, a democratic nation under
attack from nondemocratic forces, external or internal. . . . No
complicated geopolitical calculations of national interest are necessary."[49]

On the day after the invasion of Iraq was launched, Richard
Perle gloated in the *Guardian:* "What will die is the fantasy of the
UN as the foundation of a new world order. As we sift the debris,
it will be important to preserve, the better to understand, the intellectual wreckage of the liberal conceit of safety through international   law   administered   by   international   institutions."
Subsequently, in a book revealingly entitled *An End to Evil,* Perle
together with neo-con David Frum proposed[50] attacking North
Korea, Iran, Syria, Libya, and Saudi Arabia.

The intellectual biographies of the neo-cons—their evolution
as disappointed liberals, the influence of gurus like Leo Straus and
Albert Wohlstetter, the attachment of some of them to Israel—
all of this has intrigued journalists. And whatever the sources of
their ideas, the neo-cons are no doubt sincere. They are convinced
that moral imperatives drive the growth of American militarism. But it is not their sincerity which gives them access and influence. Rather it is that their vision of a righteous and armed America stamping out evil in the world provides a rationale for the
growth of the military establishment. And so far, the crusade
against evil has benefited the establishment handsomely. The military budget alone is up by 35 percent under the Bush regime,[51]
and the average annual rate of growth in spending for defense,

homeland security, and international affairs has more than tripled to 13.6 percent.[52]

WAR AND "THE BASE"

War serves another political purpose for the Bush regime. The patriotic enthusiasm and sense of national emergency that war encourages helps to paper over divisions between factions in what Republicans call "the base," the inner network of organized new right groups, some of them with far-flung grassroots constituencies, that support conservative Republicanism.[53] The groups are actually quite diverse. They have different agendas, and different ideological commitments. However, the promise of access to power is seductive, and most of them work together in loose coalitions, although their differences constantly threaten to tear apart those coalitions. The expansion of government and of government spending promoted by the military-industrial establishment, (and by important business interests like the pharmaceutical companies) strains these alliances.

The annual Conservative Political Action Conference, first convened three decades ago, is where the Republican big tent meets. It includes evangelists, antitax groups, pro-business interests, libertarians, antilabor groups, and gun enthusiasts. In January 2004 the conference honored the "fiscal heroes" who voted against the president's Medicare bill. And Bob Barr, former congressman from Georgia, denounced the administration's expanded powers as a dangerous threat to liberty, saying "We don't want a surveillance society." The president of the National Taxpayers Union called the administration's record "abysmal." These are signs of trouble that Dick Cheney tried to smooth over when he addressed the conference, talking about the "cause we all share" and emphasizing the Bush doctrine of holding foreign nations accountable for harboring terrorists.[54]

Grover Norquist, the long-time president of Americans for Tax Reform, meets regularly with presidential political brain Karl Rove, and has become a kind of machine-boss for the Bush administration.[55] Norquist hosts weekly meetings in Washington that bring together senior White House and congressional staffers, lobbyists, business leaders, gun owners, libertarians, members of the Christian right, and conservative policy experts, as well as writers from conservative publications like the *Washington Times* and *National Review*. They share an agenda of slashing taxes and rolling back government programs, including privatizing Social Security, and promoting free trade, tort reform, and school choice. Looking toward a second Bush term, Norquist recently called for the immediate outsourcing of 850,000 federal civilian jobs, to be followed by the outsourcing of state, and county city jobs, the elimination of farm subsidies, the expansion of school vouchers, and the establishment of personal savings accounts instead of Social Security.[56]

Corporations with a strong interest in rolling back government in order to rollback government regulation, such as Philip Morris, Pfizer, and Time Warner, help fund Norquist, whose boast that he aims to shrink government "to get it down to the size where we can drown it in the bathtub" acquired a certain notoriety. He calls his group the "Leave-Us-Alone Coalition." But this agenda certainly doesn't make his coalition a natural ally of the military-industrial establishment. "Wars are expensive and dangerous," he says. "They're not political winners." And he doesn't like the domestic antiterror campaign either, especially the Patriot Act, which he understands is not shrinking government.[57]

These groups on the new right do share some broad convictions. They are all fiercely anticommunist, they believe in free markets, and they couch their arguments in a shared vengeful Christian moral rhetoric. But their specific interests are not compatible. Christian fundamentalists are not libertarians; tax cutters are not natural allies of the military establishment.[58] The Bush immigration proposal that I will discuss in chapter four is similarly a source of controversy. Businesses employing low-wage workers like the leverage this proposal gives them over the immigrants who work for them since employer certification would be required for temporary work permits.[59] But the prospect of even temporarily legalizing immigrants raises fury among other groups in the base. Bush has tried to prevent these divisions from widening with rhetoric emphasizing the need to rein in federal spending, for example, and by submitting supplemental budget requests for waging war and occupying Iraq instead of including them in the regular budget. But, however described, spending continues to grow, and the immigration proposals are designed in part to try to win votes in the closely contested states where Hispanics are concentrated. As I write this in late winter 2004, cracks are beginning to show in the base. Still, the anxieties and passions aroused first by the war on terror, then by the war on Iraq, and conceivably continuing indefinitely into the future as the war on evil proceeds, tend to smooth over those divisions in the Republican base, at least so long as the sense of national emergency remains strong.

WAR AND WINNING ELECTIONS

War fever has been useful to the Bush regime in another way. It has helped win elections. The conservative Republicans who now virtually control all branches of the federal government, and many state governments as well, had to get elected and reelected. Majorities of voters had to pull the lever for Republican candidates, and a war scare helped. "Transforming frustration at home into action abroad," says Wesley Clark, "has emerged as a pattern in democracies under stress."[60]

This does not mean that American elections are fair in the absence of war. They aren't. We know that incumbents have large advantages and are overwhelmingly reelected, that district lines are redrawn to favor incumbents and the majority party, that the state and local officials who run elections make it easier for some people to vote than for others and, perhaps most important, we know that money enormously amplifies the appeals and the deceits of some candidates and not of others. The Republican fundraising advantage is now huge; the Bush-Cheney campaign chest alone is expected to raise $200 million, a record in electoral history.[61] All that acknowledged, however, both public opinion polls and electoral results show that partisan divisions in the American electorate remain precariously close for the Bush regime, and in the face of close elections, a war on terror and a war on Iraq swayed a good many people to vote Republican.

Nor does this mean that returning Democrats to power would solve our problems. The Clinton administration did preside over a reduction in the number of men and women in the armed forces, but it also conducted bombing forays over Iraq, for example, and certainly did not stand up to the military industrial establishment. But neither did it put multilateral international agreements at risk and, as I will go on to show, it was less aggressive in pursuing a business, right-wing domestic policy agenda. Our problem now is not simply to strive for a more democratic and just government. It is to ensure the survival of the international and domestic institutions that will permit the mobilization of democratic influence over the longer run.

George W. Bush assumed office under a cloud. He had lost the popular vote in the 2000 election, albeit by a close margin (and

despite extraordinary maneuvers such as the infamous Florida
purge of black voters who were presumed to be ex-felons). The
Florida vote count that gave him the electoral college votes he
needed was widely disputed because of a variety of irregulari-
ties, and so was the Supreme Court decision that finally handed
him the presidency. Moreover, he took office as the economy
was falling into recession. No wonder he was dropping in the
polls. Until May 2001, the Senate was evenly divided, with Vice
President Cheney breaking tie votes. Then Jim Jeffords, the Republican senator from Vermont, switched from Republican to Independent and announced he would vote with the Democrats.
Meanwhile, the Republicans had only a narrow majority in the
House.[62]

September 11 was a shock to American voters, and a gift to the
Bush regime. "In the hours immediately following the September
11, 2001 attacks on the World Trade Center and the Pentagon,
Secretary of Defense Donald Rumsfeld asked for plans to be
drawn up for an American assault on Iraq. The following day, in a
cabinet meeting at the White House, Rumsfeld again insisted that
Iraq should be "a principal target of the first round in the war
against terrorism."[63] And Condoleezza Rice asked senior staff of
the National Security Council to think about how to capitalize
on these opportunities to change U.S. doctrine and shape the
world.[64]

Perry Anderson writes that September 11 gave the new administration, "elected by a small and contested margin. . . . an unex-
pected chance to recast the terms of American global strategy
more decisively than would otherwise have been possible. Spontaneously, domestic opinion was now galvanized for a struggle figu-
ratively comparable to the Cold War itself."[65] On September 26,
2001, fully 90 percent of Americans said they approved of the
way George Bush was handling his job as president.[66]

Well, not entirely spontaneously. The administration seized on the attacks to recast the president and his party as the anointed saviors of America at war. The president's rhetoric was grand, and increasingly biblical as time wore on: "Just three days removed from these events, Americans do not yet have the distance of history, but our responsibility to history is already clear: To answer these attacks and rid the world of evil."[67] Robert Jay Lifton writes of this process as the "mobilization of public excitement to the point of a collective experience of transcendence. War then becomes heroic, even mythic, a task that must be carried out for the defense of one's nation, to sustain its special historical destiny and the immortality of its people."[68]

The religious overtones cannot be missed. The code name for the combat aircraft that were almost immediately deployed over the Persian Gulf was "Operation Infinite Justice," a phrase the U.S. Christian Apologetics and Research Ministry define as God's terrible price for the reinstatement of His created humanity to sin-free purity.[69] Garry Wills says that "The odd euphoria of war resembles the jubilant confession of sinfulness at the Great Awakening. We are afraid and exhilarated. The multiple items of population are drawn together into a People, God's People." Wills goes on to say that while many "have wondered how the president can so readily tear down structures of international cooperation when, in the fight against terrorism, we need them most," his apparent certainty, "hard to justify in terms of geopolitical calculus," comes from being assured that God is on our side. "Question the policy, and you no longer believe in evil—which is the same, in this context, as not believing in God."[70]

As the 2002 midterm election approached, the war on terror came to play a large role in the administration's electoral plan. The Democrats tried to make the recessionary economy the issue. But

Karl Rove, managing the campaign for Bush, knew how to foil that appeal. In a speech to the Republican National Committee in January 2002 he urged them to take political advantage of Bush's war on terrorism, arguing that the public had more confidence in Republicans when it came to national defense.[71] September 11 made it possible for the Republican machine to change the subject from the economy to protecting America from terrorists, from Iraq, from evil-doers everywhere. "There's reason to suspect," says Elizabeth Drew, "that the resolution approving war against Iraq was deliberately timed by Rove and Bush to occur just before the 2002 midterm election." Republican ads during the campaign pictured the faces of Democratic senators up for reelection alongside the faces of Usama bin Laden and Saddam Hussein. Max Cleland, Democrat from Georgia, was one of the senators exposed to this treatment. Cleland was a veteran who had lost three limbs in the Vietnam War. Nevertheless, he was defeated. And as the war propaganda continued, Iraq emerged as the enemy in American opinion. In the immediate aftermath of September 11, the overwhelming majority of Americans had believed, correctly, that Iraq was not involved. Once the administration's propaganda machine swung into gear for war, however, a majority of the public decided Iraq posed an imminent threat to American security and was planning new attacks.

The strategy worked in the 2002 elections. The Republicans gained two seats to retake the Senate and increased their House majority by six seats.[72] In March 2003, the much trumpeted attack on Iraq occurred. As everyone knows, there were no weapons of mass destruction, and there was very little armed resistance, at least during the American and British takeover. The occupation proved more difficult as insurgency continued and the American occupying forces proved unprepared for the task of occupation and reconstruction. Whether the victory proves a victory at all is still not clear. But none of this was apparent during the 2002 election.

Now the 2004 election approaches. The president and his party are exploiting all of the usual stratagems available to incumbents to protect majorities in Congress. Fewer than forty House races are judged to be competitive, and the Republican leadership is scrambling to reduce even these. They are far ahead in fundraising. Overall, the three Republican Party fundraising committees brought in $183 million in hard money during 2003 as compared to $83 million for their Democratic counterparts, and the Republican Senatorial Committee held a ten to one advantage over its Democratic counterpart.[73] The Democrats are countering with "527s," organizations named for a section of the tax code, which arguably can still collect soft money despite new campaign finance restrictions, so long as they do not communicate with party bodies. However, not only have the Republicans challenged the legality of the 527s, but they have issued a challenge so broad that it extends to any group (other than political action committees) that "promotes, supports, attacks, or opposes" any candidate for federal office.[74]

It will be especially difficult for the Democrats to overtake the Republicans in Congress. In the Senate only fifteen seats are thought to be competitive. And gerrymandering is being aggressively used to remove Democratic contenders in the House. After the 2000 census the Pennsylvania Republican legislature drew new district lines that resulted in the state's congressional delegation shifting from eleven Republicans and ten Democrats to twelve Republicans and seven Democrats in the 2002 elections. Inspired by this victory, the aggressive Republican House Majority Leader Tom DeLay planned a takeover of the Texas state legislature to achieve a similar result there. Corporate contributions were funneled to Republican contenders for seats in the Texas State House of Representatives, and the Republican majority thus elected then took the unprecedented step of redrawing district lines drastically between censuses to favor Republican candidates for Congress. With the aid of computer technology, districts were reconfigured so that as many as eight of the seventeen Democratic members of the Texas delegation to Congress could be unseated. The redistricting was sustained by a three-judge federal panel, and the new lines quickly persuaded one Texas Democrat to switch parties, while the Democrats are not even fielding a candidate in another district. "We've already picked up two seats and we haven't even had an election," boasted DeLay. DeLay's use of corporate contributions to win the Republican majority in the state legislature that made this possible is under investigation by a local prosecutor.[75]

The biggest stake in the election is the presidency. Unprecedented sums of money have been collected, new compassionate conservative initiatives are announced daily, and the Bush team is working hard to reinterpret the president's record on the economy, as when the Council of Economic Advisors recently moved back the starting date of the recession so it could be relabeled "the Clinton Recession."

But central to the reelection strategy is the effort to sustain the lift in the polls generated by the war fever, notwithstanding growing ambiguities on the ground. The chairman of the Republican National Committee even suggested that a presidential election was inappropriate at a time of war: "Senator Kerry crossed a grave line when he dared to suggest the replacement of America's commander-in-chief at a time when America is at war."[76] In his State of the Union speech in January 2004, President Bush reiterated the war theme, in phrases that echoed evangelical Christianity: "We've not come all this way through tragedy and trial and war only to falter and leave our work unfinished," he said. Commenting on the speech, David M. Kennedy, a historian at Stanford, said: "This was a remarkably candid acknowledgement of how much he intends to exploit the political value of his posture as the only effective warrior against terror."[77] And in a February 23, 2004 speech defined as kicking off his election campaign, President Bush repeatedly invoked the September 11 attacks and his leadership in war.[78] Meanwhile, the Republican National Committee has begun to screen hardball advertisements that again invoke danger and patriotism. The narrator of one ad intones: "Some are now attacking the president for attacking the terrorists. Some call for us to retreat, putting our national security in the hands of others."[79]

The war strategy may not succeed a second time. In any case, the war with Iraq may have been launched too early for a lift in the 2004 election, assuming that electoral calculations were indeed an important motive for war. A week after the State of the Union address, the president's approval ratings had fallen to 50 percent from 54 percent in the last *Newsweek* poll. And for the first time, a named Democrat beat the president in a poll about the next election.[80]

Still, our political prospects are hard to know, and alarming.

3

POWER AND PLUNDER:
IMPLEMENTING THE DOMESTIC
BUSINESS AGENDA

WAR-MAKING SHORED up the power of the Republican right. To be sure, they already controlled the presidency and the House of Representatives. After the 2002 midterm election they also regained control of the Senate, and they were on their way to controlling the federal courts. But Republican domination was precarious. The American public remained closely divided in partisan terms, margins in the House and the Senate were narrow, and surveys showed that majorities of the public were actually opposed to many elements of the right's policy agenda. War, and the fear and patriotism that war evoked, overrode this emerging political opposition. War thus not only nourished the right's allies in the military industrial complex, and galvanized the right-wing base, smoothing over its fractiousness, war fever also moved majorities of Americans to throw their support behind a president and his party who promised to lead them through their fear and their excitement to victory. War, in short, empowered the right-wing Republican leadership.

This is not an instance of the pursuit of power for its own sake. The political power of the Republican right has been delivered to the big business interests that backed the administration and its party. The fog of war also helps in this process, for national security rationales have been used to divert public attention from the huge strides that are being made in implementing the big business agenda. We usually regard imperial war as a strategy that makes possible the predation of foreign lands and peoples, or "accumulation by dispossession" in David Harvey's phrase. But in this instance war is also a strategy for domestic predation, a strategy for enacting the policies that dispossess resources and rights from ordinary Americans on an unprecedented scale. Nobel laureate in economics George Akerlof calls this "a form of looting."[1]

Even the aggressive takeover of the Iraq economy that followed in the wake of occupation will benefit business interests at the expense of the American public. The massive sums appropriated by Congress for the occupation and reconstruction of Iraq are paving the way for the creation of a neo-liberal economy under rules established by the Coalition Provisional Authority. Two hundred Iraqi state companies have been privatized under CPA Order 39, and full foreign ownership of Iraqi banks, mines, and factories is allowed, and indeed so, except for the oil industry, is the full repatriation of profits.[2] Income and property taxes have been suspended for the year, and future taxation is limited to 15 percent. Most Iraqi workers get the same $60 a month they received under Saddam Hussein, but the bonuses, profit sharing, and food and housing subsidies workers previously received have been ended. Already U.S. occupation forces have taken Iraqi union leaders into detention, and a decree prohibiting "civil disorder, rioting or damage to property" may well be aimed at increasingly desperate Iraqi workers.[3] Some American corporations will probably profit handsomely from this neo-liberal takeover. But ordinary Americans are so far footing the bill for the hundreds of billions of dollars appropriated for reconstruction and occupation. And if at some time in the future a new Iraqi government takes back their economic enterprises, American corporations will no doubt be bailed out by the U.S. Treasury and American taxpayers.[4]

These developments notwithstanding, the main targets of business looting are not in Iraq. They are within the borders of the

United States. If we step back in time, it is clear that the business political agenda now being enacted under the cloud of war is a continuation of a campaign that began three decades ago when American business became intensely politicized. To be sure, big business has always attended to politics, but rarely with the zeal and determination of the past three decades. The origins of this campaign are in the economic troubles of the early 1970s when American business was simultaneously struggling with oil price shocks, rising competition from West Germany and Japan, and the narrowing profit margins resulting from the array of labor, social welfare, and regulatory gains won by the social movements of the 1960s and early 1970s. Big business responded by mobilizing an army of lobbyists and think tanks to promote a political agenda that would shore up profits by rolling back the public policies of the New Deal and Great Society.

The main planks of that agenda were cutting taxes on business and the affluent, reducing government regulation of business, weakening unions, and slashing the public programs that shored up the power of workers, largely by reducing the pain of unemployment. The agenda gained considerable traction under Ronald Reagan, another president who enjoyed the overwhelming support of big corporations, as well as the support of a right-wing populist base of Christian fundamentalists, gun advocates, tax cutters, and libertarians first activated in reaction to the civil rights and women's movements of the 1960s and 1970s. The Reagan administration was partially successful in rolling back regulatory and social welfare programs. Reagan took office at the beginning of 1981 and by summer, Congress had approved cuts of $140 billion in federal social programs covering the years 1982–84, more than half from income maintenance programs for the poor. New investment and depreciation tax write-offs were introduced that favored the largest corporations, and personal income and estate taxes were slashed with most of the benefits going to the more affluent. And new administration directives reduced environmental and workplace regulations, while budget cuts weakened their enforcement.[5] As with the Bush administration, Reagan also succeeded in spurring a large military buildup. But many of the programs that the Reagan Republicans were trying to whittle back were popular, Reagan appointments to the Environmental Protection Agency were soon mired in scandal, and unlike the Bush regime, the Reaganites did not control the House of Representatives or the federal courts. Eight years of Reaganism essentially produced a standoff, especially with regard to popular environmental measures and the biggest social programs: Social Security and Medicare.

There were of course some Reagan successes, and in any case, with the rising influence of business and the proliferation of business-backed think tanks, the business agenda became mainstream and even bipartisan political wisdom, embodied in the doctrine sometimes called neo-liberalism, and more recently called the Washington Consensus. The main planks have changed little over thirty years: lower and less progressive taxation, reduced government regulation, reduced government spending on social programs, and the privatization of public programs wherever possible. The Carter and Clinton administrations moderated the program, but they were not exceptions to its basic thrusts, and especially not exceptions to the neo-liberal principle of "deregulation of all markets" as the impetus to more economic activity."[6] The Clinton administration controlled government spending stringently, championed a draconian welfare reform, and repealed a good deal of financial regulation, even as it presided over the bailouts of Mexico in 1995, and Long Term Capital Management in 1998.[7] But these were limited neo-liberal initiatives compared to what has followed. The Bush administration has taken advantage of the public support generated by war to push forward strenuously on the business policy agenda.

TAX CUTS AND DEREGULATION

Perhaps the most alarming policy changes for the longer term occurred in the tax system. After all, effective government depends on revenues, and the Bush administration has moved rapidly to deplete public revenues. In 2001, the president pushed tax cuts through Congress amounting to $1 trillion over ten years. Then in 2003, with the war in Iraq under way, another huge tax cut was enacted, amounting to $800 billion over ten years. Income taxes were reduced by an estimated average of $90,000 per millionaire,[8] the federal estate tax on large inheritances was phased out, the rate on capital gains was cut from 20 percent to 15, and the top rate on dividends was slashed from 39.6 percent to 15 percent. Corporate taxes were allowed to wither as a source of federal revenue through new generous write-offs for investments in plants and purchases of equipment that will total more than $175 billion through 2004, and much more if they are not allowed to expire in a few years as is now expected.[9]

War proved to be a bonanza for the president's tax plan. "Republicans are discovering," said the *New York Times* on March 23, 2003, "that the conflict can provide a new tool of persuasion. . . . House leaders pounded home the idea that it was not the time to embarrass the president by defeating his budget plan." The same strategy also prevailed in the Senate. "When our troops are over there fighting, we don't want partisan bickering to be what they see on television back home," said Senator Kay Bailey Hutchison,

Republican from Texas. "We want them to see our support, our total commitment, because if the economy sags, it's going to affect everyone over there fighting now."[10]

The president's 2005 budget continues the campaign with a proposal that families be allowed to shield as much as $30,000 yearly on their investment income, effectively abolishing any remaining tax on such income.[11] The budget also calls for forty-two new subsidies in the form of tax cuts for "everything from health insurance to decommissioning nuclear power plants."[12] All told, the new tax cuts proposed in the 2005 budget came to another $737 billion over ten years, according to the Congressional Budget Office.[13]

The federal tax cuts in turn have had a ripple effect on state revenues. Many states link their personal and business income taxes to the federal tax system, so state tax receipts fell by at least $10 billion, and this after years of state-level tax cuts during the booming 1990s that had deprived state treasuries of more than $40 billion a year. The federal tax cut legislation did include, as a result of pressure by Senate moderates, $20 billion in fiscal aid to states. But the amount was paltry compared to the deficit the states confronted of perhaps as much as $200 billion in 2003 and 2004 combined.[14]

The president repeatedly justifies the tax cuts as an economic stimulus necessary to generate jobs and economic recovery. The 2001 tax cut legislation was called the Economic Growth and Tax Relief Reconciliation Act; the 2003 tax cut legislation is the Growth, Jobs, Opportunity Act. But tax cuts for the affluent are unlikely to have the effect of stimulating the economy and job creation. "Although financial reporters have started to realize that Mr. Bush is out of control—he has 'lost his marbles,' says *CBS Market Watch*—the sheer banana-republic irresponsibility of his plans hasn't been widely appreciated," writes Paul Krugman.

"That $674 billion tax cut you've heard about literally isn't the half of it. Even according to its own lowball estimates, the administration wants $1.5 trillion in tax cuts over the next decade."[15] *Reuters* reported on April 2, 2003, the president had met with thirteen economists who expressed unwavering support for the tax proposals, especially the cuts in taxes on dividends. No wonder; these were Wall Street economists. Some 450 prominent economists, including ten Nobel laureates, disparaged the plan.

The broad pattern in these tax cuts is apparent. "If you take the administration's tax proposals as a group," says Krugman, "they effectively achieve a longstanding goal of the radical right: an end to all taxes on income from capital, moving us to a system in which only wages are taxed—a system, if you like, in which earned income is taxed but unearned income is not."[16] In other words, the historic progressivity of the modern income tax, always justified on the simple rationale that the well-to-do should pay a larger share of their federal taxes than the rest of us because they can afford it, is being eliminated. "Another significant tax cut could be enough to eliminate progressivity from the U.S. tax system" says economist Brian Roach from Tufts University.[17] The flat tax, long promoted by the right, is on its way. And to worsen the impact of these legislative changes, there is the growing problem of what the General Accounting Office calls "abusive tax-avoidance schemes" that are proliferating rapidly and which the IRS itself estimates to cost the government tens of billions of dollars. David Callahan reports that tax evasion now costs the U.S. Treasury at least $250 billion annually, "and probably much more."[18] Of course, tax avoidance and evasion schemes are not new, but they are undoubtedly encouraged by the antitax political campaign of this administration.[19] Notice that the IRS has been starved of resources for enforcement; if the administration's 2005 budget proposals are enacted, the agency will see its budget for modernization cut from $388 million to $285 million.[20] In any case, the agency has been so whiplashed by attacks in Congress that it investigates the returns of working-class households that receive Earned Income Tax Credits much more closely than those of high-income taxpayers, so the big tax evaders go largely unpunished.

An obvious consequence of the new tax laws is that the tax burden is shifted from the rich to everyone else. Corporate income tax revenues fell to $132 billion in 2003, down 36 percent from $207 billion in 2000, representing only 1.2 percent of the Gross Domestic Product and the lowest level since 1983, a year in which corporate tax receipts fell to levels last seen in the 1930s.[21] Meanwhile, the share of federal revenues consisting of payroll taxes rose to the highest level in the nation's history.[22] But the consequences go beyond the redistribution of the tax burden.

Falling revenues and rising deficits are significant for another reason important to the right-wing agenda: they generate enormous pressure for cuts in spending, especially cuts in spending on social programs. Overall federal revenues as a share of the economy are falling sharply to their lowest level since 1959, while federal deficits are ballooning. "Except during the two world wars, the fiscal reversal amounts to the largest four-year deterioration in the federal budget in American history. . . . Since the present administration took office, the foreign indebtedness of the United States has increased by $1.4 trillion."[23] And fully half of that deficit was the result of the Bush tax cuts.[24]

Dick Cheney is reported to have said that Reagan proved deficits don't matter, meaning they don't matter to the voters. Reagan in fact proved that deficits do matter to Congress, if only because they can be used as a club to press for cuts in social programs. The tax cuts have already reduced revenues by $270 billion in 2004. This is barely a beginning, since most of the cuts have not yet taken effect. Indeed, only 11 percent of the cuts will take effect before 2008, and revenues will fall far more as the full impact of the administration's tax cuts unfolds. Over ten years, an estimated $12 to $14 trillion will be lost, more than enough to pay for the Social Security and Medicare shortfalls combined.[25] "It will be a perfect fiscal storm" said Leslie B. Samuels, a partner at Cleary Gottlieb Steen & Hamilton, who served as assistant secretary for tax policy under President Clinton.[26] The anticipated fiscal storm has led even the International Monetary Fund to worry about the long-run fiscal stability of the United States.[27] The storm could well suck up the money that might otherwise be spent on our major social programs. Paul Krugman calls this "the bait-and-switch strategy known on the right as 'starve the beast.' The ultimate goal is to slash government programs that help the poor and the middle class, and use the savings to cut taxes for the rich."[28] Federal Reserve Chairman Alan Greenspan, has already "raised a red flag about Social Security, warning that federal deficits, already large, would begin to explode after the first wave of baby boomers becomes eligible for Social Security benefits four years from now, and for Medicare three years after that."[29] Greenspan supported the tax cuts and now endorses the administration's effort to make them permanent. He called on Congress to solve the problem by cutting back Social Security benefits.[30] What is being contemplated, in other words, is in fact the repudiation of government debt, but not the debt held by foreign creditors. Rather it is the debt held by the American public that would be repudiated.

The political path for the massive tax cuts was smoothed in part with deception, deception that began before war was declared and continued afterwards. The Bush administration described its tax policies as a deserved reward to middle class and working Americans. In a radio address on February 3, 2001, Bush said: "The country has prospered mightily over the past twenty years. But a lot of people feel as though they have been looking through the window at somebody else's party. It is time to fling the doors and windows open and invite everybody in. It is time to reward the work of people trying to enter the middle class and put some more money in their pockets at a time when they need it. . . . Above all, my plan unlocks the door to the middle class for hardworking Americans." And Ari Fleischer, White House press secretary, followed suit a few days later on February 5: "In terms of who will have their life changed the most by a tax cut, it's clearly the people at the low and middle end of the income scale, because this represents a huge surge in their income."[31] The White House website reiterated these distortions, claiming, for example, "In 2003, 91 million taxpayers will receive, on average, a tax cut of $1,126 under the Jobs and Growth Act of 2003."

But "average" was deceptive, since it averaged the $93,000 savings of the 184,000 millionaires making more than $1 million a year with the far more numerous taxpayers who save much less. Understandably, the public is befuddled by such claims.[32] In fact, 84 percent of taxpayers will get less than the average. Had the White House used the median, the number that divides the population in half, the amount would have been a tax cut of about $217.[33] Meanwhile, the problem of looming deficits was reduced in the 2005 budget proposals by the simple expedient of leaving out or understating the costs of a number of the administration's initiatives. Defense spending is understated, for example, the costs for the occupation and reconstruction of Iraq are omitted, as is the cost of fixing the alternative minimum tax, a change widely agreed to be necessary that is expected to drain the budget of $600 billion over the next decade.[34] The Office of Management and Budget, which customarily estimates federal revenues and deficits over ten year periods, released estimates for the fiscal years

2003 and 2004 which were limited to a five-year projection, thus eliminating the revenue losses that would accrue as the tax cuts were phased in over time. The Department of the Treasury cooperated as well, releasing distribution tables that departed from the usual practice of showing how much money would be gained or lost by each income category, and providing data only on percentages gained or lost.[35]

The excitement over war, the boost it gave the president, was important in pushing through the tax cuts. "Never before in wartime," writes Holly Sklar, "with Americans killed, wounded and captured in the line of duty, have the wealthy lined their pockets with tax breaks."[36] But this time, war was invoked as the justification for tax cuts that lined the pockets of the rich. The Republican leaders of the House waved the flag and talked about war as they rallied the votes they needed. And when George W. Bush raced to Ohio to try to pressure a stubborn Senator George V. Voinovich to support his tax plan, he made a point of visiting the only producer of the Abrams M1-A1 and M1-A2 tanks that American forces used in Iraq as he "pivoted in one paragraph from the war against Saddam Hussein to the American economy" and, presumably, the need for tax cuts.[37] This was a curious and historically anomalous sort of politics. The administration invoked patriotism to push for tax cuts that would benefit the affluent, even while it was also beating back attempts to improve soldiers' pay or improve veterans' benefits.

*   *   *

Deregulation is also high on the corporate agenda. Much of this has been accomplished under the radar, through complex and little-noticed changes in regulations, or in amendments to legislation, or in funding, or through court decisions by judges who are

increasingly sympathetic to the administration's agenda. Molly
Ivins grasps the pattern: "Take any area— environment, labor, education, taxes, health—and go to the websites of public-interest
groups in that field. You will find page after page of minor adjust-
ments, quiet repeals, no-big-deal new policies, all of them cruel,
destructive, and harmful. A silent change in regulations, an executive order, a funding cutoff."[38] When the Environmental Protection Agency denied a petition to ban the disposal of sewage
sludge as fertilizer, it did so on New Year's Eve, not a likely time to
get news coverage.[39]

Environmental deregulation has been especially important,
partly because it is important to the ever-more-powerful energy
lobby, including the oil, gas, coal, nuclear, and utility industries.
The energy industry has been lavishly generous to politicians.
"Since 1998, oil, gas and related services companies on the Fortune 1000 list gave $13.9 million to Republicans, compared to
$3.2 million to Democrats," although it should be pointed out
that the industry takes no chances, and does contribute to Democrats, and hires Democratic as well as Republican lobbyists.[40] The
Bush-Cheney campaign in 2000 was treated especially generously,
receiving some $165,672 from oil and gas companies on the For-
tune 1000 list, $250,000 from the coal industry and $225,950
from the nuclear industry.[41] And at least twenty-two energy executives and their spouses are either Pioneers or Rangers in Bush's
reelection campaign. Pioneers collect or donate $100,000;
Rangers pledge $200,000. When the *New York Times* added up all
the contributions by particular political action committees and individuals to federal candidates, and soft money contributions to
the parties for the 2000, 2002, and 2004 election cycles, it reported that coal-fired utilities like Southern Company had contributed $3,971,337 with 72 percent going to Republicans; TXU
contributed $2,250,049 with 77 percent going to Republicans;

First Energy Corporation of Akron, Ohio, $2,081,522 with 72 percent going to Republicans. Meantime, the top lobbyists managing these relationships were also top Republicans, including Haly Barbour, former head of the National Republican Committee, G. Boyden Gray, White House counsel during the first Bush administration, and Marc Racicot, soon to become chairman of the Republican National Committee.[42]

Once in office, the Bush administration rewarded its energy industry supporters. Vice President Cheney convened a secret but soon-to-be notorious Energy Task Force which was revealed to have had 714 contacts with energy industry insiders and only 19 contacts with conservationists and other outsiders. The Sierra Club and Judicial Watch sued Cheney to reveal who had participated in the meetings: Theodore B. Olson, the U.S. solicitor general, argued that it "would violate fundamental principles of separation of powers" to force the president or the vice president to disclose with whom they had met, and the case made its way to the Supreme Court. Before the case was heard, Supreme Court Justice Antonin Scalia traveled as Cheney's guest on an Air Force plane to hunt ducks in Louisiana, to a fair amount of chortling in the press.[43] Despite the ensuing furor, and the ripostes of late-night comedians, Justice Scalia has refused to recuse himself from the case.[44] In the meantime, a lawsuit taken by the Natural Resources Defense Council and Judicial Watch produced a ruling in a federal district court requiring the Bush administration to release documents related to the closed-door meeting.[45]

The sweeping energy bill that resulted from the Cheney task force is now stalled in Congress, but what it offers the industry is revealing, a veritable cornucopia of subsidies, tax breaks, and regulatory rollbacks that revise existing environmental measures, especially the Clean Air Act. Some examples: royalty payments for oil wells on public lands are eliminated; the petroleum industry is offered legislative protection against lawsuits over a cancer-causing gasoline additive known as MTBE that has leached into groundwater in hundreds of communities; tax breaks for the energy industry are estimated at about $23.5 billion by the Congressional Joint Committee on Taxation, and the industry gets another $5.4 billion in grants, subsidies, and loan guarantees; $6 billion in tax credits for the nuclear power industry; the exemption of oil and gas construction activities from the Clean Water Act; the exemption of drilling companies from the Safe Drinking Water Act; reimbursements to oil and gas companies for the cost of environmental impact studies; the removal of the authority of the secretary of the interior to deny applications to drill on public lands; weakened regulations governing utility mergers and the repeal of the Public Utility Holding Company Act of 1935 that shielded consumers and investors from Enron-like business maneuvers.[46]

Whether the bill becomes law or not, it reveals the administration's exceptional solicitousness toward the industry to which it is most closely tied. And the Bush regime has in any case moved ahead to take care of the industry by executive fiat or by more specific legislative initiatives. As Bruce Barcoff says, while the administration's legislative initiatives "have languished on Capitol Hill, the administration has managed to effect a radical transformation of the nation's environmental laws, quietly and subtly, by means of regulatory changes and bureaucratic directives."[47] The first move was the abandonment of the Kyoto Protocol and with it the international effort to curb global warning. Former Treasury Secretary Paul O'Neill, commenting on his participation in that decision, said that no one cared about the facts, about the tradeoffs entailed, because "energy concerns and . . . industry lobbyists had eclipsed considerations about action on global warming."[48] Afterwards, President Bush tried to put a publicly acceptable gloss on the decision by proposing voluntary industry reductions of global warming gases. A *Washington Post* survey found that as of January 2004 a mere fifty-four American companies had agreed to participate.[49] And in March 2004, scientists at the Mauna Loa Observatory in Hawaii reported that levels of carbon dioxide, the gas largely responsible for global warming, had been growing at an accelerated pace in the past year, reaching record levels.[50]

George W. Bush actually campaigned in 2000 as something of an environmentalist. When Bill Clinton vetoed legislation approving the Yucca Mountain project for disposing of nuclear waste, Bush seemed to approve, releasing a statement after the veto that said "As president, I would not sign legislation that would send nuclear waste to any proposed site unless it's been deemed scientifically safe."[51] As president, Bush approved the Yucca Mountain Project which, beginning in 2010, will become the storage site for 70,000 metric tons of spent nuclear fuel. And he also proposed expediting licensing for nuclear reactors and expanding the generating capacity of existing plants.

The Bush administration has initiated other environmental rollbacks that favor the energy industry, including new rules regulating mercury emissions from power plants (an examination of the text of one of the three proposed rules revealed that at least a dozen paragraphs were lifted, sometimes verbatim, from industry suggestions).[52] Implementation of some of the changes to the Clean Air Act relaxing the rules governing emissions from aging coal-burning plants was suspended by the courts in December 2003 when fourteen states sued the Environmental Protection Agency to block the policy.[53] Now the administration is pressing ahead with an alternative plan to let power companies swap their rights to release mercury.[54] The 2004 defense authorization bill of $401.3 billion signed into law in November 2003 exempts the military from abiding by the Endangered Species Act and the Marine Mammal Protection Act.[55] In the winter of 2003–2004, the administration introduced initiatives to allow electric utilities to delay fifteen more years before decreasing mercury emissions and to open the North Slope in Alaska to oil drilling. The Bush administration has also sharply slowed the pace of cleanups of contaminated sites by the Superfund program, and reduced the funds of the program by one-third in inflation-adjusted dollars since 1993.[56] Bush also took Greenpeace to court for protests against illegal logging and his administration has continued to stonewall on the issue of climate change.[57]

Just as this regime's business support reaches far beyond the energy industry, so do its giveaways. Access to public lands has been eased by executive fiat not only for oil and gas exploration, but for commercial logging interests, under the banner of what the president calls his Healthy Forests initiative."[58] In April 2004, the administration eliminated a rule that required federal agencies to survey Pacific Northwest forests for rare species and to establish buffers to protect them, a change that could open thousands of acres of old growth forests to logging.[59] The president's 2005 budget proposals reduce the EPA allocations for waste treatment and other clean water activities by 30 percent.[60] The new legislation providing limited drug benefits for seniors under Medicare is laden with gifts for the pharmaceutical and health insurance industries, including subsidies for the private insurers that will offer the drug benefits, an arrangement that is widely perceived as a foot-in-the-door strategy to encourage privatization of the entire Medicare program. The legislation also guarantees the pharmaceutical industry that the new program will not result in any government pressure to lower drug prices.

Drug manufacturers will gain about $139 billion in extra profits, showing that the $60 million they've dispensed in political contributions, and the $37.7 million they've spent on lobbying, was wisely invested.[61] Jim Hightower reports that Marc Racicot, the chairman of the Republican National Committee, wrote to the giant drug company Bristol-Myers Squibb enclosing the drug benefit legislative proposal, asking if Bristol-Myers would like to make changes and requesting a $250,000 contribution to the party.[62] And now the administration has proposed a new Medicare chief, Dr. Mark B. McClellan, who as head of the Food and Drug Administration led opposition to any change in federal law that would make it easier to import lower-cost prescription drugs. "We want to know" said Senator Byron L. Dorgan, Democrat from North Dakota, during the confirmation hearing, "why the FDA has embarked on this crusade. It's supposed to regulate, not represent, the pharmaceutical industry."[63] And Senator John Kerry, now the Democratic nominee for the presidency, said he wants to "allow individuals, pharmacists, wholesalers, and distributors to import FDA-approved prescription drugs from other countries at lower prices." He added that "the only reason George Bush has opposed this approach is that the drug industry would lose billions in profits." Under fire, Dr. McClellan backed down, and agreed that he would work with Congress to assure the safety of prescription drugs imported from Canada.[64] Meanwhile, for the second time within a year, the White House launched an effort to impose strict caps on jury awards in medical malpractice suits. The earlier effort in the summer of 2003 would have imposed a $250,000 cap on jury awards for pain and suffering in all medical malpractice cases. This time the effort was limited to capping awards in suits against obstetricians and gynecologists. This is part of a larger administration crusade for tort law reform backed by doctors and business groups, and resisted by consumer advocates and trial lawyers. The new measure was defeated, for the time being. "We're going to keep going until we succeed," said Senator Elizabeth Dole, Republican of North Carolina.[65]

No major industry backer of the administration seems to have been neglected. Big media is another important example. From ClearChannel's rallies to censoring war criticism to beating the drums for war, media companies have lent the administration enormously important support. And the administration has attempted to reward them. The main media rules that have been at issue are the prohibitions against newspaper-broadcast cross-ownership; limits on the number of TV stations one media company can own nationally and locally; and a rule that prevents a company from owning TV stations that together reach more than 35 percent of the population. The traditional justification for these rules, says Robert McChesney "was based on the idea that the government was granting firms beachfront property in the media system when they were given monopoly licenses to broadcast channels. Therefore the public had an interest in preventing firms from monopolizing these scarce licenses and dominating the media system."[66] The White House wants to relax these rules and to that end appointed Michael Powell, an advocate of deregulation and especially of relaxed ownership rules, to head the Federal Communications Commission, the watchdog agency.

In the spring of 2003, top broadcasters worked with Federal Communications Commission officials to prepare the rules that would relax media ownership. According to the Center for Public Integrity, FCC officials met with representatives of the industry seventy-one times, and with the top media moguls, not just with lobbyists. And on June 2, 2003, the *Wall Street Journal* disclosed that the new rules had been drafted with the aid of a Wall Street media stock analyst. Ron Wyden, Democratic Senator from Oregon, observed that loosening ownership rules "rings the dinner bell for big media corporations who are salivating to make a meal out of the nation's many small media outlets."[67] In this case, and largely as a result of the efforts of dissident commissioners, the

new rules aroused a small storm of controversy, provoking something like a citizen's movement of opposition, including opposition from groups in the Republican base offended by what they
consider the vulgarity of big media and concerned also about
the atrophy of local media. Remarkably, considering that the
big media corporations add to the power gained from lobbying
and campaign contributions their ability to control the news and
the public depiction of politicians, Congress reacted with efforts
to override the FCC and again lower the ownership limit to 35
percent. Then the president threatened a veto, and the Republican leadership was able to keep the measure off the floor. John
Nichols reports that Rupert Murdoch's news operations, already
massive, particularly benefited from the new rule.[68]

In February 2004 the Bush administration and its congressional allies, along with cooperating Democrats, were working on
a Senate bill called The Protection of Lawful Commerce in Arms
Act that would grant legal immunity to gun manufacturers and
dealers from liability suits, as long as they did not sell defective
weapons or violate the law. The bill is the gun industry's response
to proliferating lawsuits from municipalities and the state of New
York charging gun makers and dealers with responsibility in criminal shootings.[69] The gun lobby has already gotten a provision, in-
serted in an omnibus spending measure, that requires federal
officials to destroy records on gun purchases within twenty-four
hours instead of waiting ninety days.[70] Republican efforts to
shield the gun industry are a kind of "two-fer"; since protection
of the industry also resonates with the pro-gun populist agenda of
the powerful National Rifle Association which is so important in
the right-wing base. Senate Democrats managed to get some Republican support for including amendments in the bill that would
extend existing legislation banning assault weapons and requiring
background checks of customers at gun shows. The amendments

were regarded as "poison pills" by promoters, and the bill was defeated. The National Rifle Association, which had made immunity for gun manufacturers and dealers one of its highest legislative priorities, is threatening revenge at the polls.[71]

In the fall of 2003, on a Friday afternoon when no one was paying attention, the Department of the Interior reversed a Clinton-era ruling and decided that companies mining precious metals can use as much federal land as they want to dump the substantial wastes they produce.[72] The food industry has been very effective in getting top Bush officials to approve products before their safety can be established. A senior scientist at the Department of Agriculture said researchers there were pressured by the agriculture secretary to approve cattle from Mexico at risk of tuberculosis, pears from China with fungus infections, as well as boneless meat from Canada.[73] The Bush administration also killed regulations that Clinton officials were developing to reduce the risk of Listeria infections from poultry.

The mad cow episodes in the winter of 2004 prompted Ann Veneman, the secretary of agriculture, to appoint a panel of international experts to make recommendations about appropriate measures to protect against the disease. The panel has already made it clear that the only realistic way to contend with the threat is to bring our handling of meat and meat by-products up to international standards. The testing is now voluntary, and only 40,000 head of the 35 million cattle slaughtered annually are tested.[74] The National Cattlemen's Beef Association is counterattacking.[75] Meanwhile, the Japanese have refused to accept American beef exports without the sorts of testing safeguards that are now used in Europe, and at least one major beef producer, Creekstone Farms in Kansas City, has suggested its willingness to test. "The problem we're having now," said John Stewart, Creekstone's president, "is that the USDA is not wanting to do this. They don't want to recognize B.S.E. is a problem." Spokespersons from the Department of Agriculture said they would respond when the department has completed its evaluation, which would take awhile.[76] In January 2004, the department did ban meat from "downer" cattle (cattle too sick to stand) for human consumption and raised its testing goal to 40,000 animals. The advisory panel recommended an increase to 221,000.[77]

The sugar lobby is also being placated. American sugar is not competitive globally, but it competes very well indeed in Washington and succeeded in facing down Australian demands for access to American sugar markets.[78] And now, for a second time, the administration is trying to get an exemption for more American farmers from an international ban on the use of methyl bromide, a pesticide that damages the ozone layer. "It is the first time any country has proposed to reverse the phase-out and increase the production of a chemical that is supposed to be eliminated," said David Doniger from the Natural Resources Defense Council.[79]

Needless to add perhaps, these are not science-backed initiatives. Robert F. Kennedy Jr. details the chilling instances of the Bush administration's deliberate manipulation and misrepresentation of the scientific findings even of its own agencies, as well as the political stacking of scientific committees.[80] After 9/11, numerous press releases by the EPA reassured the public that the air quality in downtown Manhattan was wholesome, and that asbestos dust levels were either absent or very low, even though the EPA's own data did not support that conclusion. A respected microbiologist with the Department of Agriculture, who had found dangerous antibiotic-resistant bacteria in the air surrounding industrial-size hog farms, was ordered not to speak out publicly, an order prompted by lobbyists from the National Pork Producers Council. The administration has simply discredited a dozen major government studies on global warming, as well as a report by the Intergovernmental Panel on Climate Change, no matter that the measurements by U.S. government scientists showed rapid increases in levels of carbon dioxide, the main cause of climate change, for three successive years.[81] When EPA scientists found the process of extracting oil and gas known as hydraulic fracturing contaminated groundwater supplies in violation of federal standards, they revised their findings in congressional testimony, explaining the change was based on "industry feedback." Interior Secretary Gale Norton substituted findings from an oil company for findings from the Fish and Wildlife Service on the effects of oil drilling on caribou in the Arctic National Wildlife Refuge. Tommy Thompson, secretary of Health and Human Services, acknowledged that his agency had altered a report on racial disparities in health services to give the report a more positive cast.[82] When National Fisheries scientists changed their findings on the impact on salmon of diverting water from the Klamath River to benefit agribusiness supporters, some 34,000 fish died, which environmentalists say is the largest fish kill in the history of the west.[83] EPA stalled on releasing a report on the disastrous impact of mercury on children's health, presumably as a favor to the coal and utility industries whose mercury discharges are dangerous in the immediate locales of the utilities. And what the EPA would not do, the White House did. White House staff rewrote or deleted information accompanying new EPA-developed regulations for coal-fired power plants, information largely drawn from a 2000 report by the National Academy of Sciences that Congress had commissioned to settle the scientific disputes about the risks of mercury.[84]

The American Public Health Association protested the emerging pattern of the abuse of science as early as 2002, officially declaring that it objected to "recent steps by government officials at the federal level to restructure key federal scientific and public health advisory committees by retiring the committees before their work is completed, removing or failing to reappoint qualified members, and replacing them with less scientifically qualified candidates and candidates with a clear conflict of interest."[85] *Science* magazine, in an editorial signed by ten prominent American scientists, also railed against the Bush administration's political abuse of scientific committees.[86] In January 2004, the National Research Council of the National Academies said that air-quality laws are inadequate to prevent the pollution that threatens the environment and human health. Then, in February 2004, some sixty influential scientists, including twenty Nobel laureates, issued a statement saying the Bush administration "had systematically distorted scientific fact in the service of policy goals on the environment, health, biomedical research and nuclear weaponry at home and abroad."[87] The administration, said a *New York Times* editorial, has "belittled, misrepresented, altered or quashed" such warnings.[88] In April 2004, the White House issued a detailed rebuttal to these charges that Dr. John H. Marburger III, science advisor to the president, said were false and "preposterous."[89]

Other regulatory changes cannot be obscured with fake science. The Bush regime has pleased all of its corporate contributors, including the small business lobby, with its rollbacks of labor rights. And to the extent that this also results in smaller and weaker unions, there is the not insignificant added benefit of undermining major Democratic supporters. President Reagan made his mark as an antiunion fighter by firing striking air controllers. President Bush has adopted a similarly militant antiunion stance. In fact, the administration assault on union rights began almost the moment he assumed office and before the issue of national security could be invoked. In February 2001, the new president issued executive orders that ended labor-management partnerships in the federal government, barred project-wide collective bargaining agreements on federally funded public works projects, and required federal contractors to post notices advising workers of their right *not* to join a union.

Similarly, and almost immediately on taking office, the administration attacked workplace safety rights. It reversed the ergonomics rules that were developed (after much delay) by the outgoing Clinton administration after many years of lobbying by organized labor. A year later the administration announced a new ergonomics program based on industry-specific voluntary guidelines. Meanwhile, it slashed the budget of the Occupational Safety and Health Administration, repeatedly sought increased funding to audit and prosecute unions, and announced plans to put up to 850,000 federal jobs up for bid to private contractors. And now it is attempting to change overtime rules by raising the income ceiling for guaranteed overtime, a good thing but only for some 800,000 workers, while also reclassifying millions of other workers as high-level administrative or professional employees. An estimated 7 to 8 million private-sector workers could lose overtime pay as a result of the reclassification being proposed. In addition, on-the-job or military training could be substituted for advanced degrees in deciding whether white collar employees are ineligible for overtime pay. The existing test of whether an employee exercises "independent judgment" would be replaced with the test of whether the worker is in a "position of responsibility," a test which at least arguably could exempt employers from paying overtime to most workers.[90]

After September 11, national security became a favored argument for rolling back labor rights. In December 2001, only a few short months after 9/11, the president appointed a Presidential Emergency Board and imposed a sixty-day ban on job actions by the 15,000 machinists at United Airlines. In October 2002 he directed the Department of Justice to seek a Taft-Hartley injunction to end an eleven-day shutdown of the west coast docks. This was the first time in American history that a president in effect allowed an employer to lock out workers, and then rewarded the employer with court-ordered government intervention. It was also the first time the Taft-Hartley Act has been invoked since 1978.

On January 7, 2002, the president issued an executive order revoking union representation for employees working in a number of divisions of the Department of Justice, presumably on security grounds. In June 2002, the president issued an executive order stripping the nation's air traffic control system of its designation as an "inherently governmental" function, opening the door to privatization and threatening the representation and bargaining rights of 15,000 controllers. Then in the fall of 2002, Bush threatened to veto the legislation creating the Department of Homeland Security unless it stripped the 170,000 federal employees of the agency of their civil service and union protections, again on homeland security grounds, of course. Senate Republicans even undertook a filibuster to defend the administration's position, which ultimately prevailed. In January 2003, the administration issued a directive denying collective bargaining rights to the 60,000 newly federalized airline security screeners, invoking the war on terrorism to justify the move, and it also terminated the collective bargaining rights of workers at the National Imagery and Mapping Agency. And discussions are now beginning about a National Security Personnel System that would affect the collective bargaining and employee appeal rights of some 700,000 civilian employees at the Pentagon.[91]

The reenergized campaign against labor took its toll among private-sector workers as well. In March 2004, labor suffered a defeat in a major dispute involving 138,000 striking supermarket workers in California who were trying to protect their health benefits and ward off a two-tier contract that would pay newly hired workers less than current workers.[92] A January 2004 government report showed that union membership fell again last year by 400,000 workers. Just 8.2 percent of private-sector workers now belong to unions, down from 60 percent two decades ago.[93]

The Bush administration has presided over historic revelations of systematic fraud across corporate America and Wall Street. Similar revelations in earlier periods produced a rash of new regulations of business and finance. This time, scandal produced mainly a few indictments. A number of those fingered in the scandals were important Bush contributors, most notoriously Kenneth Lay of the Enron collapse. Indeed, The Center for Public Integrity calls Enron the top career patron of George Bush, and Enron executives of the reorganized company continued to contribute to the Bush campaign in 2003, long after the scandal broke.[94] Enron manipulations purportedly cost investors $70 billion, and cost Enron workers heavily as well in jobs and life savings lost. Lay used a loophole in securities laws to secretly sell some $80 million of Enron stock, even while he was urging Enron workers to keep buying Enron stock. So far, not much has happened. To be sure, Martha Stewart was indicted and her trial was given a great deal of publicity. But Martha Stewart was a small-time player, charged with a maneuver that saved her about $50,000 and she may not have been guilty in any case. Doug Henwood reports the Wall Street banks, at the heart of the chicanery, mostly got off with a $1.4 billion settlement deal with the authorities, less than 4 percent of their profits over a four-year period. As the *Wall Street Journal* headlined a story reviewing the events, it was the "Year of the (Shrugged Off) Scandal."[95]

War fever obscured the multiple ways that the Bush regime was the agent for business plunder. Tax cuts, new subsidies, and deregulation were, after all, outright grabs at the expense of the public sector and public well-being. But there was another less direct aspect of the campaign, the attack on social programs that had been developed over the course of the twentieth century to moderate the hardships of the unregulated market. I turn to this aspect in the next chapter.

POWER AND PLUNDER: ROLLING BACK SOCIAL SPENDING

THE BUSH REGIME has taken up the long-term business campaign against American social programs. These are the programs that improve the well-being of people who earn little or nothing, or that provide services such as education or health care that cannot be left to the market. The campaign against social spending has been stoked by the growing acceptance of the classical conservative justification for middle class resentment, particularly of the programs for the poor, recently summed up by David Brooks in a diatribe against the Great Society: "In reality, culture shapes economics. A person's behavior determines his or her destiny. If people live in an environment that fosters industriousness, sobriety, fidelity, punctuality and dependability, they will thrive. But the Great Society welfare system encouraged or enabled bad behavior."[1]

Bush himself has echoed this view. "The new culture," he wrote, referring presumably to the liberalization of the 1960s, "said if people were poor, the government should feed them. If criminals are not responsible for their acts, then the answers are not in prisons, but in social programs. People became less interested in pulling themselves up by their bootstraps and more interested in pulling down a monthly government check. A culture of dependency was born. Programs that began as a temporary hand up became a permanent handout, regarded by many as a right."[2]

The popularity of these attitudes acknowledged, employers have been the most consistent opponents of the social programs.

Redistribution through government taxation and spending is an issue for them, but it is not nearly as important as the impact of the social programs on labor markets. The underlying problem is longstanding. To the extent that the social programs reduce economic insecurity among workers or potential workers, workers acquire a measure of independence and therefore of power in their relations with employers. When the pain of unemployment is eased through cash grants to the jobless, for example, all workers are less anxious and less likely to kowtow to their bosses, and the unemployed in particular are less desperate for any job at any wage. They are also a little less desperate and a little less vulnerable to employers when wages from work are supplemented by government housing or health care or nutritional subsidies.

More recently, another business interest in social programs has emerged, and it is becoming important. Notwithstanding the sharp cuts that have been made in some programs, large sums of money continue to flow through them, and inevitably will continue to flow through most social programs. That money has been targeted as a new frontier for business profiteering. The campaign to privatize social programs is unfolding in education, welfare, job training, and most importantly because so much money is involved, in Social Security and Medicare. The Bush administration is working to push this campaign forward.

Employer opposition to social spending is longstanding. It was overcome in the United States only during periods when popular economic discontent reached levels that threatened both civil order and the stability of reigning political regimes. During the Great Depression of the 1930s, joblessness and hardship led to demonstrations and riots across the country and also led to the defeat of the then-dominant Republican Party. Programs like emergency relief, and later Social Security and unemployment insurance, were initiated quickly by Franklin Delano Roosevelt to deal with the immediate threat of popular unrest, and to build long-term support for his New Deal Democratic coalition. Once trouble subsided, however, most of the social programs atrophied, until a new surge of popular protest erupted in the 1960s, this time spearheaded by the civil rights and urban poverty movements. The New Deal programs were revived and expanded, and new programs were added, most importantly Medicaid and Medicare. It is worth noting that at these peak moments of crisis in the 1930s and 1960s, even leaders of big business supported new social spending.

The business political mobilization that began in the 1970s, however, targeted the New Deal and Great Society programs for rollbacks, partly to justify the tax cuts business was demanding, but more importantly as a component of the effort to roll back labor costs. The reforms advocated by the new business-backed think tanks like the Heritage Foundation and the Manhattan Institute were actually a revival of formulae that have existed since the days of poor relief, and were applied most assiduously to the means-tested programs which reach the poor: welfare, food stamps, and Medicaid. Eligibility for benefits, said the reformers, should be more strictly conditioned by work and marital behavior, real benefits should be lowered, states should have a larger role in the administration of benefits, bureaucratic discretion to give or withhold benefits should be increased, and wherever possible, the privatization of the programs should be promoted. Ironically, these features actually go part of the way toward explaining popular antipathy toward the means-tested programs. Low benefits and intrusive procedures stigmatize both the programs and their beneficiaries, and this cultural stigma is then mobilized in attacks on the programs.

The long-term campaign against social spending has been reignited by the Bush regime. The campaign proceeds not through big and flamboyant new proposals but through the step-by-step erosion of the programs. The Center on Budget and Policy Priorities titled a review of the cuts proposed by the president in 2001 and 2002 "Left Behind in Good Times and Bad" to make the point that cuts for low-income programs were proposed in 2001 when large surpluses were predicted, and again a year later after tax cuts and a recession. The president's proposals during recession would have decreased low-income programs (apart from education) by about $3 billion, or nearly 5 percent.[3] This pattern persisted in the budgets for 2004 and 2005, and the 2005 budget also proposes spending caps on all discretionary programs, except of course for defense and homeland security. Moreover, the longer term Office of Management and Budget projections show that after 2005 the cuts in domestic programs will grow larger each year through 2009.[4]

Let me illustrate the overall pattern by showing how the campaign against social spending affects particular programs. Since the New Deal, the Aid to Families with Dependent Children (AFDC) program, known as welfare, provided cash assistance to low-income families, primarily families headed by women. Clinton-era legislation replaced AFDC with Temporary Assistance for Needy Families (TANF), which came up for renewal in 2002.

In 2004, the president proposed a series of changes in TANF that would require states to force more of the mothers remaining on the rolls to work in exchange for their benefits—up from 50 percent to 70 percent—and also require them to work a full forty-hour week. What counts as work would also be defined very narrowly so as to curtail not only access to education, but even participation in state drug abuse and vocational training programs intended to overcome barriers to employment. And the president also wants to divert limited program resources to marriage promotion projects. At the same time, although recipients would be working more hours, the Republican leadership has resisted increased child care appropriations, and this despite a dire shortage even now, before the increased work requirements are implemented. Only one in seven of eligible and needy families actually receive child care help.

So far, the proposals have been stalled, partly on the issue of child care appropriations, and instead Congress has merely extended the existing program. This year, however, an aggressive move led by Representative Wally Herger, Republican from California, tried to insert a formula into the extension that would achieve the president's objectives by increasing work requirements through a backdoor adjustment. The new formula would raise the work requirements by recalibrating the credit toward filling work participation quotas that states now receive for cases that are removed from the rolls.

The technical details of the Republican proposals to one side, they seem to be animated by a crusading harshness. After all, the welfare program had already been effectively eviscerated as a result of the decades-long campaign that culminated in the 1996 welfare reform law that established TANF. The Clinton-era law introduced stiff work requirements and strict time limits on the receipt of benefits, and not only turned over administration of the program to the states, but did so with a block grant arrangement that gave the states a strong fiscal incentive to reduce the number of families that received aid, simply because the states in effect kept the money they didn't spend.[5] Predictably, the states made welfare much harder to get, and harder to keep, and the rolls plummeted. Only the most vulnerable families with hard-to-employ mothers, whether because of disabilities or substance abuse or dire family problems, remain on the welfare rolls, and it is they who will be affected by the new work requirements. Meanwhile, and despite rising unemployment and job loss reports, the Republicans have only slowly and reluctantly extended unemployment benefits.

The current budget proposal also fails to extend a provision in the 2001 tax law that provided a tax credit to working families with incomes below $50,000 to encourage pension savings. The tax cut legislation already gives generous breaks to wealthier tax-payers for such retirement savings. And the 2003 tax cuts accelerated the tax cuts enacted in 2001 for high-income families, without any tax benefit for low-income families, just as it accelerated "marriage-penalty relief" tax cuts for high-income married couples, but not for low-income married couples.[6]

As the number of low-wage workers increases and cash assistance through welfare shrinks, the Earned Income Tax Credit (EITC) becomes more important. The program provides refundable tax credits, meaning cash, to supplement the wages of low earners. Begun under Nixon, the program has gradually expanded, usually with bipartisan support. After all, it would seem hard to oppose modest assistance to low-wage workers and their families. But beneath the radar of public attention, eligibility screens are being contemplated that are likely to drive people out of the EITC program. New IRS regulations would target some families who file for the EITC—stepparents, foster parents, single fathers, grandparents, aunts, and so on—and require them to pre-certify by producing birth certificates, marriage licenses, or whatnot by December 31, months before they normally file tax returns. This is a catch-22 arrangement that will make it less likely that many families will apply. First-time applicants won't know they have to pre-certify. Many people will find the required documents hard to obtain. And the December 31 deadline ignores the fact that the commercial tax preparers on whom many people rely usually don't open before the beginning of the year.[7] Meanwhile, a resolution introduced in the Senate by Republican Don Nickles, chairman of the Budget Committee, would cut EITC appropriations by $3 billion over five years.[8]

Unemployment insurance is also a cash assistance program. The main program is run by the states and paid for with payroll taxes. But since eligibility under the regular program is ordinarily limited to twenty-four weeks, the federal government usually appropriates funds to provide benefits for the longer-term unemployed when jobless levels are high. The current federal program began to phase out in December 2003. Meanwhile, a total of 3 million jobs had been lost during the Bush term, and from late December to the end of February 2004, an estimated additional 760,000 workers exhausted their regular unemployment benefits. With an election approaching, the legislation to extend the unemployment insurance program will probably eventually be agreed to. That it has been stalled and resisted is, however, worth noting. So are the arguments being made. The economy is said to be improving so benefits are no longer needed, no matter that few jobs have been created so far in this upturn. And then there is the familiar argument against cash and in-kind assistance, that they weaken the incentive to work. In this vein of reasoning, federal unemployment benefits prolong joblessness by reducing the unemployed workers' incentive to find a job.[9]

It is not only cash assistance programs that are being chipped or hacked away. So are programs that provide in-kind benefits. In a move reminiscent of President Reagan's proposal that ketchup be classified as a vegetable in school lunches, the School Lunch Program is now under fire by the Bush administration. Responding to a media report of a study that claimed 27 percent of the children in the program were actually ineligible, the administration proposes to require documentation of income levels from all applicant families to reduce fraud. Of course, most of the supposedly ineligible families were in reality families for whom documentation was incomplete, which was not surprising given language barriers and the complexities of low-income life on the one hand, and the carelessness of staff on the other. But extensive documentation requirements will succeed in cutting children from the program. The Center on Budget and Policy Priorities estimates that the campaign to require documentation will keep over 2 million eligible children from receiving free or reduced-cost meals.[10]

Low-income housing subsidies were first targeted for large cuts by the Reagan administration. In the years since, housing costs have escalated much more rapidly than the overall rate of inflation, but wage rates have not, with the result that housing costs absorb a larger and larger share of the earnings of lower-income people. Now the Bush administration is attempting to make this problem worse by proposing measures to cut what remains of our low-cost housing programs. The main target is the housing voucher program known as Section 8, initiated under the Nixon administration to help low-income families bridge the difference between what they can afford and rental costs in the private market. The program now serves about 2 million poor households, which is only about one-quarter of the eligible families, and has a long waiting list. Last year the president's budget proposals would have underfunded the program by about 180,000 vouchers. Congress did not implement the cuts, and the administration's effort to turn the program into a state block grant went nowhere last year. This year's budget tries to slash the program again, by more than $1 billion and by $1.6 billion if the amount of funding needed to maintain current levels of service is taken as the standard.[11] This could mean that 250,000 fewer families will receive assistance, and it is the first time in the history of the program that the number of vouchers would be reduced.[12] The administration is pursuing the block grant path as well with a flexible voucher proposal to turn the program over to public housing authorities. The general idea seems to be to replicate the 1996 welfare changes in the housing provisions, and accordingly, time limits on housing subsidies are also being discussed, no matter that time limits on housing subsidies, by forcing families to move or even making them homeless, would create devastating instability in the lives of these families, with inevitable consequences for work and school. Other proposed changes would remove regulations that were intended to ensure vouchers would reach the poor, and this at a time when census data show growing shortages of affordable housing for extremely low-income renter households, a majority of whom now pay more than half of their income for rent.[13]

The Medicaid program that provides health insurance for low-income people is also under assault. The program was initiated in 1966, and is financed and administered jointly by the federal and state governments. The late 1990s were a period of especially fast growth, partly because, after the big Clinton health plan was defeated, that administration tried to make some incremental progress in health care by expanding coverage under Medicaid, primarily to children in families just above the regular Medicaid eligibility levels. There were also promises made to expand Medicaid as a kind of compensation for the fact that Clinton had signed the welfare cutback legislation of 1996. By now, the Medicaid rolls include 47 million people, at a cost of $265 billion.

Medicaid—and health care problems generally—have remained in the political spotlight partly because the number of people without health insurance coverage has continued to rise and now stands at more than 43 million. One reason is job loss, especially the loss of better-paid manufacturing jobs that were more likely to provide health insurance. It is also because rising health insurance costs have prompted more and more employers to demand employees pay part or all of the health insurance bill. When, as is often the case, workers simply cannot afford this, they lose their insurance. In 2002 the Bush administration made a gesture of responding to the problem with a program called the Health Coverage Tax Credit, which was supposed to help workers who lose jobs and health care coverage because of foreign imports. The program was seen as a prototype, a solution that could be expanded to more and more of the uninsured population. Tax credits would pay for 65 percent of the health insurance premiums of a displaced worker. But since the monthly cost of premiums has now risen to several thousand dollars, most displaced workers simply cannot afford them, tax credits or not.[14] The program, not surprisingly, is sputtering, and health insurance scams by companies that offer cheap coverage, collect premiums, and then refuse to pay claims, are proliferating.[15]

The Bush administration's current plan for Medicaid is circuitous. Basically, they want to turn the program into a block grant, thus setting a limit on federal expenditures which would not rise as the states enroll people, and also ceding the states more authority over the program, making it easier for states to cut back on services such as prescription drugs or nursing-home care. This is broadly what block grants meant in welfare. This year, the administration proposes a rather devious scheme of financial aid to the states, offering the financially strapped states $3 billion in loans for Medicaid next year, and $13 billion over seven years, but only if they agree to pay back $10 billion in the subsequent three years, and only on condition that they agree to block grant the program.[16] Bush administration officials are also taking the block grant fight to the states. On February 20 the *Nashua Telegraph* reported that Governor Craig Benson, Republican of New Hampshire, was asking Secretary of Health and Human Services Tommy Thompson to make his state the first to block-grant its Medicaid program.

With these proposals pending, the Bush administration is pursuing other measures that will increase the pressure on state Medicaid budgets. It is cracking down on state methods of financing their share of Medicaid costs, arguing that states have used creative bookkeeping ploys to get large amounts of federal Medicaid money. Now the Bush administration is promising to impose strict federal oversight on state Medicaid budgets. The president's 2005 budget actually claims $1.5 billion in savings next year, and $23.5 billion in the next decade, as a result of these efforts.[17] Meanwhile, the budget reduction proposals by Senator Don Nickles referred to earlier would reduce Medicaid spending by $11 billion over five years.

Some of the administration's proposals involve so little money and seem so gratuitously mean-spirited they are puzzling. In his 2003 State of the Union message, the president boasted of a new $450 million program for mentoring the children of prisoners. His budget proposals shortly afterwards allocated $150 million, and also eliminated a number of other programs that reached those same children, with the result that there was an overall reduction of $39 million.[18] And despite the obvious problem of after-school care, especially for working parents, the 2004 budget proposed to reduce other after-school services for children by $400 million.

*　　*　　*

The logic that threads through these social program initiatives is the logic of the labor market. Programs are being refashioned to make long hours of low-wage work the only option available to many. Even the vein of meanness contributes to this logic, for it heaps insult on those who turn to government support. The Bush administration immigration initiatives should also be understood in this way. Most immigrants, including legal immigrants, were already denied eligibility for the main means-tested programs under the 1996 welfare law. Although these measures might have gained some political traction among anti-immigrant groups from the belief that such restrictions would keep immigrants out, they did not, and neither did Congress show much appetite for the strong border controls that might keep immigrants out. To the contrary, our de facto policy seems to be to allow immigrants in—albeit not easily—and to deny them the protections that might allow them to defend themselves from low-wage employers.[19]

The president's new immigration proposal is consistent with that policy. To be sure, it would give temporary legal status to undocumented workers for three years, with the possibility of an extension. This tenuous legalization will be promoted by the administration in its appeal to Hispanic voters. But under the plan, prospective immigrants would have to have a job waiting, and they would have to keep it once they were here. It is only employers who can obtain permits for legal guest workers, and the permit belongs to the employer. Undocumented workers already here could be admitted to the program, but only if their employer sponsors them. Workers will be bound to their employers by the threat of losing their temporary legal status and deportation. As Mike Davis says, the "Bush proposal, which resembles the infamous Bracero program of the early 1950s, would legalize a subcaste of low-wage labor without providing a mechanism for the estimated 5 to 7 million undocumented workers already in the United States to achieve permanent residence or citizenship. Toilers without votes or permanent domicile, of course, represent a Republican utopia. . . . a stable, almost infinite supply of indentured labor."[20]

There are ample precedents for this sort of policy, extending back to the nineteenth century when immigrants from Europe and Asia were often brought here by labor contractors. But the more recent precedents are in guest-worker programs for Mexican workers.[21] The most notorious was the Bracero program initiated during World War II to bring in Mexican workers to help harvest the fields. To make sure they would not stay, a part of their salary was deducted, presumably to be given back when they returned home. It rarely was, and that along with the harsh treatment of the migrant workers, earned the program a reputation as a form of peonage. The Bush proposals, which tie workers to particular employers, could also create a form of peonage.[22] No wonder that business executives in the low-wage hotel, restaurant, hospital, construction, and agriculture industries are cheering. "Americans just don't want to take a lower-paying, entry-level job," said Frank Romano, founder and owner of the Essex Group, a chain of fifteen nursing homes and assisted-living facilities. They will not apply for it. Last year I had to spend close to $300,000 on help-wanted ads because it was such a struggle to find people to do the jobs we need done."[23]

John Sweeney, president of the AFL-CIO, talked about the same reality but put it in a different light. The president's proposal, he said, would create "a permanent underclass of workers. . . . The plan deepens the potential for abuse and exploitation of these workers while undermining wages and labor protections for all workers."[24] Representative Bob Menendez, Democrat from New Jersey, had even stronger words. He called the plan "a glorified guest-worker program with no new path to legalization." While Bush, he said, "wants their sweat and labor, he ultimately doesn't want them. The proposal will be a rotation of human capital, to be used and discarded, with no hope of permanently legalizing one's status."[25]

Of course, the president and his party are not talking about the labor market aspects of his proposal. Rather the theme is inclusiveness; Bush is reaching out to Hispanic voters, at least with rhetoric and ritual. The new immigration proposals were announced in a speech delivered in the White House to an audience of Hispanic leaders who jammed the room. "For a party that's trying to look more inclusive and welcoming, the proposal has broader thematics that show an openness to America's new immigrants," said Bill McInturff, a leading Republican pollster.[26]

*   *   *

In the United States, the federal government shares responsibility for many social programs with state governments and sometimes with county or city governments as well. The trumpeting of the Bush No Child Left Behind legislation notwithstanding, education remains primarily a state and local responsibility. Cash assistance to the poor originated as a local program, and today welfare and Medicaid are a shared responsibility. The federal government pays part of the cost and establishes basic rules, but the programs are largely administered by the states, and state revenues pay for part of their costs as well. Moreover, the private nonprofit or voluntary social services play a large role in the United States in the care of the disabled, the aged, and in the provision of health services, and states and localities foot much of the bill.

The federal role in social spending dates from the 1930s when, under the Social Security Act, the national government initiated grants-in-aid to the states and counties to provide cash assistance to the aged, the disabled, and orphaned children. The Social Security Act also prompted the states to initiate unemployment insurance programs. Shortly afterwards, a federal program to aid localities that provided low-cost public housing was introduced. In the 1960s, the federal role expanded, as new federal grants-in-aid were created, and the federal government assumed direct responsibility for programs like Medicare, as well as nutritional supplements.

Since the 1970s, the Republican–business opposition to social spending has taken the form of attacking the federal role under the banner of devolution. The argument is that state and local governments are closer to the people, and therefore better suited to run these programs. The argument is specious, for several reasons. Decision making in state and local bodies is typically even more inscrutable than at the federal level. Moreover, after many decades when the federal government took the initiative on social programs, the organized groups that advocate for the programs have relocated to Washington, and are less prepared for the state-by-state politics that devolution requires. And finally, there is the long-standing problem of the structural vulnerability of state authorities to the threat of business disinvestments, which helps account for the leverage that business exerts in state policy decisions. This is the main reason that state governments are so ready to offer subsidies to companies contemplating new investments. Estimates of the total costs of these giveaways range from $30 billion to $50 billion a year. "It seems like almost every state is giving away grandmother, grandfather, the family jewels, you name it, everything," said Alan Peters, a professor at the University of Iowa who tried to estimate the costs of subsidies across the country.[27]

The constraints that lead states to subsidize business are also evident in patterns of state taxation, which are steeply regressive, with the top 1 percent paying a lower rate than everyone else. According to the Institute on Taxation and Economic Policy, the top

1 percent paid just 5.2 percent of their income in state and local taxes in 2002, while middle-income households paid 9.6 percent, and those with incomes under $15,000 paid 11.4 percent.[28] During the exuberant 1990s, most states cut taxes, and they cut taxes especially on business and the better off.

Regressive state and local taxes in turn encourage middle- and working-class groups to perceive themselves as abused taxpayers. And the resentment is heightened by the fact that class is conjoined with race, ethnicity, and gender in the United States. Since many of the poor who are most at risk of needing the social programs are likely to be minorities or women, racial and gender animosities combine with tax resistance to fuel resentment of social spending, especially at the state and local level.

This is the context in which the impact on the states of the Bush tax- and social-spending cuts should be examined. The federal tax cuts reduced state revenues because state tax formulas were hitched to federal tax formulas. At the same time, flagging employment and a weak stock market caused further revenue losses, combining with tax cuts during the 1990s to produce huge state deficits that totaled about $190 billion from 2001 through 2003, and are estimated at an additional $40 to $50 billion in 2004.[29] In the past, budget crises on the state level have usually been moderated by increases in federal grants. This time they were aggravated by cuts in federal grants, and by the imposition of new unfunded mandates on state governments by the federal government, including the requirements of homeland security,[30] of the Help America Vote Act, and the No Child Left Behind law.

Meanwhile, the practice of short hospital stays is shifting the prescription drug costs of the elderly and the disabled from Medicare, a federally funded program, to Medicaid, to the tune of an estimated $28 billion during the course of the state fiscal crisis.

The Center on Budget and Policy Priorities estimates that from state fiscal year 2002 through fiscal year 2005 federal policies will cost states and localities a total of about $185 billion.[31]

Some states have tried to cope by raising taxes, but they did so through formulas which fell heavily on low- and moderate-income families. In any case, state politicians are resisting new taxes, for the usual reasons. In California, Governor Schwarzenegger declared, as he presented a budget to deal with a $14 billion deficit, "I am a strong believer that increasing taxes will hurt our economy."[32]

Inevitably, states are coping with their fiscal shortfalls by cutting social spending. Some twenty-five states made cuts in Medicaid or in the State Children's Health Insurance Program (the extension of Medicaid to cover children in families near poverty) in fiscal 2003, and eighteen states made cuts in fiscal 2004. Texas cut $428 million in child health care and coverage was ended for nearly 170,000 children and parents of working-poor families. Minnesota cut $350 million in health care for low-income children and their parents, terminating coverage for 38,000 people. Schwarzenegger proposed $2.7 billion in cuts in social service programs, including a cap on enrollment in California's Healthy Families program.[33] An estimated 300,000 children are being put on waiting lists.[34] In fiscal 2003, seventeen states added or increased co-payments for health care under these programs; in fiscal 2004 some twenty-one states began to do the same. Overall, between 1.2 and 1.6 million people are expected to lose coverage, and half of them are children.[35]

Seniors and the disabled are also being hard hit. Oregon and Oklahoma ended their "medically needy" programs, which aid low-income people when their high health expenses cause their disposable income to fall below Medicaid eligibility levels. And Washington, Tennessee, Massachusetts, Louisiana, Missouri,

Kentucky, and Wisconsin have all tightened up on medical assistance to the low-income aged and disabled.[36]

States are also squeezing spending under TANF.[37] At least thirty-two states have limited eligibility for child care subsidies for low- and moderate-income families, and waiting lists are growing. Ohio cut $268 million in child care assistance so that 18,500 fewer children received care. Tennessee simply stopped accepting child care applications from families not receiving TANF cash assistance.

Bush will campaign as the education president. And the No Child Left Behind legislation did result in increased federal funds for local schools (although in a ruse typical of this administration, the new budget now calls for eliminating or cutting back more than a dozen other education programs).[38] No Child Left Behind required changes in local schools that cost money, and the president's promises to pay for these changes fall far short of federal appropriations, by an estimated $9.4 billion in 2004 alone.[39] Given the fiscal squeeze in the states, the pressure on education budgets is acute. Nine states cut K–12 education funding in 2003, and eleven states made cuts in 2004. Georgia, for example, cut $156 million in K–12 education funding, and in Oregon, more than fifty school districts shortened the 2002–2003 school year by up to twenty-four days. In Colorado, 1,900 fewer children will attend pre-kindergarten as a result of cuts. In Georgia, the state's reading program and class-size reduction effort for grades four through twelve have been suspended. Massachusetts has also eliminated class-size reduction and cut school breakfast programs, early childhood education, and remediation programs for high school students.[40] The states are also cutting their funding of public higher education, with the consequence that tuition at public colleges and universities is skyrocketing, rising by double digits in many places.[41]

*   *   *

Finally, there are the really big prizes, the huge Medicare and Social Security programs that have been targeted by the Republican
right from the beginning of its campaign against the social programs in the 1970s. The programs are well-defended because they
are so popular. Social Security itself is often called the "third rail"
of politics. The popularity of the programs is owed in no small
measure simply to the fact that they help a lot of people and are
not means-tested, and thus involve none of the humiliating rituals
of certifying need, of investigation and surveillance, that charac-
terize means-tested programs. Indeed, Social Security is widely
believed to be a social insurance system, a misapprehension that
was in fact carefully cultivated by the proponents of the program
during its early years in the 1930s. And then there is the fact that
both programs have huge constituencies of supporters among the
tens of millions of seniors or soon-to-be seniors who receive benefits.

These facts have bred caution among opponents of the programs. No one proposes to do away with them. Rather the argument for change is always on the ground that the programs are
financially unsound and need to be restructured in order to be
saved. And the main solution proffered is privatization. In other
words, the conservative animus against these programs is forged
not only from their general animosity toward social spending, but
with an eye to the profits that privatization promises (profits for
health care providers and insurance companies in the case of
Medicare and for Wall Street in the case of Social Security).

There are in fact financial problems looming for Medicare,
which provides federal health insurance for 41 million of the
aged, and some of the disabled, and is paid for by a combination

of payroll taxes, general revenues, deductibles, and co-payments. The financial problems expected in the future are not simply the result of demography, of the aging of the baby boomer generation and longer life spans, but are more importantly the result of anticipated continuing increases in health care costs.[42] In other words, the Medicare program is affected by the crisis in health care costs that affects all Americans. The Bush tax cuts, by depleting future revenues, of course make this problem much more serious. The recently passed Medicare Prescription Drug Act takes steps toward a market solution to this at least partially manufactured crisis. Well, not really a market solution. Rather, the legislation moves us further toward the creation of an unregulated market in health care, but a market saturated with public funds. The legislation contains subsidies for just about everyone in the health care business, including doctors, hospitals, insurance companies, and for-profit health plans. Moreover, as noted earlier, the legislation forbids Medicare from bargaining with the pharmaceutical companies to bring down the cost of prescription medicines.

More than that, the legislation contains what may be important pilot programs toward the privatization solution. Private health plans are offered $12 billion in subsidies to compete with traditional Medicare, and also guaranteed that no HMO will be paid less for a patient than the traditional fee-for-service in what is called an experiment that will be launched in six major cities in 2010.[43] Tax-Free Health Savings Accounts are introduced, which are really another tax cut for the better off. And a provision in the legislation requires that a crisis be declared if more than 45 percent of Medicare funding is expected to be drawn from general revenues in a seven-year budget projection.[44] As for prescription drugs for seniors, the bill provides an oddly patchy and limited solution. A senior will have to pay $3,600 out of the first $5,100 in annual costs of drugs before the government starts reimbursing costs.

It is noteworthy that the Bush administration and Republican leaders in Congress were determined to pass this legislation. As Elizabeth Drew reports: "Republicans allowed no House Democrats and only two Senate Democrats, Max Baucus and John Breaux, both of whom supported the Medicare bill, to participate in the House-Senate conference setting its final terms. It had been passed by the House by a five-vote margin (220 to 215) just before 6:00 A.M., after the Republican leaders made extraordinary efforts to persuade reluctant members—a process that took three hours rather than the usual fifteen minutes for a roll-call vote. Republican House leaders made offers of campaign funds to reluctant conservatives; they also threatened one Republican, who was planning to retire, with cutting off money for his son, who was running to replace him. This sort of rough stuff is without recent precedent."[45]

There were big political reasons for the rough stuff, one being the big contributions rolling in to the Republicans from the pharmaceutical companies and the HMOs. Another was the steps toward privatization that the legislation took by rolling back government's role in health care. And then there was the prospect of trumpeting the achievement of the prescription drug benefit legislation in the coming election campaign. Since the election would occur before the legislation was implemented, seniors would not have the opportunity to assess for themselves just how much of a benefit they would actually receive.

Social Security is far and away the biggest prize among the social programs, and it will also be the hardest to grab. The program was initiated during the crisis of the Great Depression, when massive unemployment and its politically destabilizing effects made

public solutions imperative. As high levels of unemployment per-
sisted, resistant even to the upturn of the economy in 1934, New
Deal politicians were persuaded that it was important to remove
the aged from the labor market. They were also helped to reach
that conclusion by the huge numbers of the aged who were mobilizing behind Francis Townsend in a movement that demanded
pensions far more generous than Social Security would ever pay.
Gradually, and especially during the 1960s, eligibility for Social
Security expanded, and benefits rose. And as these improvements
occurred, the program became very popular indeed. Then the tide
turned, largely under the influence of the business mobilization of
the 1970s, and especially of the think tanks that were created with
business money. Several arguments against the program emerged.
One was that the old were greedy, using funds that should be
spent on the young. Another was that old age itself had changed:
people lived longer and were healthier, and so they should work
longer. And finally, there was the argument that over the long run,
the program was not financially sound.[46]

Some changes were introduced. The age at which people become eligible for Social Security is being gradually raised, from
sixty-five to sixty-seven. Those currently receiving benefits who
were prohibited from working in the original legislation are now
encouraged to work by regulations that reduce the penalties on
earnings. These changes reveal that the labor market preoccupa-
tions that animated efforts to reduce other social programs also
affected Social Security.

But the Bush agenda for Social Security is far more ambitious.
Social Security was originally a pay-as-you-go system, where payroll taxes collected each year funded the pension benefits that were
paid each year. That changed in 1983 when the large deficits created by the Reagan tax cuts and defense increases were eased by a
big increase in payroll taxes for Social Security. The result is that at

least on paper, Social Security reserves have become enormous, although in actuality, those reserves exist only as treasury notes, debts of the federal government to the fund. Nevertheless, the existence even in principle of huge public pension funds is ideologically offensive to the right. More than that, were the funds converted to private pensions, a new frontier of millions of individual stock accounts and broker fees would open for Wall Street investment firms, an arrangement naturally favored by the financial firms that backed Bush, including Merrill Lynch & Co., Credit Suisse First Boston, UBS Paine Webber, and the Goldman Sachs Group, who together with others formed a lobbying group called the Coalition for American Financial Security.[47] The strident and insistent talk of a long-term crisis in Social Security financing is the overture to proposals for privatizing the system. Almost as soon as he assumed the presidency, Bush appointed a commission to make recommendations regarding Social Security. The commission concluded in December 2001 that any reform of the program should "include a system of voluntary personal accounts."[48]

George Bush has long advocated that younger workers be allowed to set aside part of their Social Security tax payments for private investment accounts. This would be a first step toward the big goal of privatizing the system. There are huge obstacles such a strategy has to overcome. One is simply that the much-hyped crisis in Social Security financing is at most a far-off and unpredictable event. Thanks to the steep increase in payroll taxes inaugurated in 1983, the system is sound for the next seventy-five years, and even after that the gap in financing is small relative to the economy, less than three-quarters of 1 percent of national income.[49] If there is a fiscal crisis looming in the foreseeable future, it is a crisis of overall federal debt and the prospect arises that the treasury notes now owed to the Social Security fund will not be honored. Another obstacle is that the step-by-step strategy of partial privatization, while honoring existing pension promises, means sharply higher costs, since the money redirected to private accounts would come out of the funds now used to pay current retirees.[50] But the largest obstacle is that the program has staunch voter support.

So, what does Social Security have to do with war? Or for that matter, what does social spending generally, or tax cuts, or deregulation, or corporate giveaways, have to do with war? Well, virtually nothing, and that is just the point. "The American public, transfixed by the unfolding invasion of Iraq, may someday look up and discover too late what the Republican Congress did while the world's attention was elsewhere. Led by the Bush administration, the House and Senate are about to march under the public's radar screen and lead the country into a decade of budgetary disaster," the *New York Times* editorialized as the invasion of Iraq began.[51] The *Times* was right. War was and is a power strategy, and for awhile at least, it smoothed the way for the implementation of the right-wing domestic agenda. Can the strategy succeed over the longer run?

DELEGITIMATION,
OR THE LEAKING BUSH BALLOON

THE BIG QUESTION, not only for Americans but for people across the globe, is whether a domestic political strategy based on war-making can succeed over the long run. In this chapter, I argue there are good reasons to think the wars that initially strengthened the administration's hand also make it vulnerable. One reason is that as the fighting continues, in Iraq, in Afghanistan, and elsewhere in Europe and Asia where terrorist assaults are spreading, the tangled and bloody consequences become more evident. This is not the quick strike and quick withdrawal to the cheers of newly liberated populations that the administration promised. These troubled developments in turn have encouraged press and congressional scrutiny of the multiple deceptions that were used to justify war-making. Finally, the administration's policies of domestic plunder contradict a well-established historical pattern. Governments undertaking war usually try to compensate their people for the sacrifice demanded of them by expanding popular political and social rights. This government is doing the reverse.

The Bush regime continues to rely on war to mobilize political support. In January 2004, the president declared to Tim Russert in a *Meet the Press* interview that he was a "war president" and used the word "war" thirty-three times in the one-hour interview.[1] In early March the Republicans kicked off what the *New York Times* said was "expected to be not only the most expensive and sustained, but also the most precisely focused advertising campaign in presidential history."[2] The first ads featured dramatic footage of the destruction of the World Trade Center towers, and a president portrayed as the resolute commander-in-chief of a nation at war. "By taking the battle to the terrorists," said Bush's campaign manager Ken Mehlman, "[Bush] has made Americans safer at home."[3] Shortly afterward the president joined New York Republican officials in a groundbreaking ceremony for a Long Island memorial to September 11 victims, and Republican ads went on the air to attack Democratic presidential contender John Kerry as "wrong on taxes, wrong on defense," and weak in "defending America." In one commercial, Bush told voters they face a choice between going "forward with confidence, resolve, and hope" or turning "back to the dangerous illusion that terrorists are not plotting and outlaw regimes are no threat." Later in March, a new Bush television ad tried to discredit Kerry by attacking him for voting against the $87 billion bill that financed operations in Iraq and Afghanistan.[4] Then, on the eve of the first anniversary of the bombing of Baghdad, Bush boasted in a speech in Fort Campbell, Kentucky, the base of the 101 Airborne Division that had lost sixty-five soldiers in Iraq, "in one year's time, Saddam Hussein has gone from a palace to a bunker to a spider hole to jail."[5] Meanwhile, Vice President Cheney also entered the contest, launching a blistering attack on Kerry, saying he was weak, inconsistent, and a threat to national security.[6] Bush advisers frankly acknowledged they intend to keep the campaign focused on September 11 and its aftermath, events which they described as the defining moments of the Bush presidency.[7]

Hermann Göring, Luftwaffe commander, speaking at the Nuremberg Trials in 1946, wondered "Why should some poor slob on a farm want to risk his life in a war when the best he can get out of it is to come back to his farm in one piece? Naturally, the common people don't want war." Göring knew the answer to the question. "But after all it is the leaders of the country who determine the policy, and it is always a simple matter to drag the people along, whether it is a democracy, or a fascist dictatorship, or a parliament, or a communist dictatorship. . . . Voice or no voice, the people can always be brought to the bidding of leaders. That is easy. All you have to do is tell them they are being attacked [and] denounce the pacifists for lack of patriotism and exposing the country to danger."[8]

The president followed Göring's age-old formula for leading a people into war. He told Americans they were in danger, that we "must not ignore the threat gathering against us. Facing clear evidence of peril, we cannot wait for the final proof—the smoking gun—that would come in the form of a mushroom cloud."[9] And on the eve of the deployment of American troops in Iraq, the president asserted that "intelligence gathered by this and other governments leaves no doubt that the Iraq regime continues to possess and conceal some of the most lethal weapons ever devised."[10]

It is not always as simple as Göring claimed, however. As war drags on and costs mount, the emotional rush of fear and patriotism fades. The arguments for war become less compelling, and so do the leaders who make the arguments, especially if the war is not going well. We were told before the war in Iraq, writes Jonathan Schell, that by now the troops would be coming home, that "Iraq's large stores of weapons of mass destruction would have been found and dismantled; the institutions of democracy would be flourishing; Kurd and Shiite and Sunni would be working happily together in a federal system; the economy, now privatized, would be taking off; other peoples of the Middle East, thrilled and awed, so to speak, by the beautiful scenes in Iraq, would be dismantling their own tyrannical regimes."[11]

Instead, at least 135,000 American troops remain in Iraq, and the American troops have suffered roughly 9,000 casualties so far. Escalating violence gives credence to those who argue that more troops should be sent into the war zone, a move that will be politically costly for an administration boasting of the success of its Iraq invasion.[12] The death toll of American troops which seemed for a time to be declining as the soldiers were pulled back to their garrisons, is rising again as insurgents develop wilier tactics.[13] In any case, the death toll among Iraqis, especially Iraqis seen as cooperating with the United States, is rising and many thousands have been killed, particularly in bombing and shooting attacks on police and army recruiting stations.[14] Abu Ghraib, Iraq's most feared prison, was nearly emptied in the last days of Saddam's regime. But now it is filling up again, with a reported 13,000 Iraqis imprisoned by the American occupation, and revelations of abuse and torture by American forces at Abu Ghraib and elsewhere, have shocked the world.[15] Robert Fisk says that Iraqi employees of the UN have fearfully removed the "UN" designation from their unmarked vehicles.[16] "The innocent Iraqi casualties," the *New York Times* editorializes, "are literally countless because the Pentagon refuses to estimate their number."[17] In March 2004, a car bomb destroyed a hotel and apartment building in central Baghdad, killing seven and injuring fifty-five. Other bombing attacks on Iraqi hotels followed quickly after, with yet more casualties.[18] In March, ferocious gun battles broke out in the Iraqi town of Falluja, a Sunni stronghold, killing Americans and Iraqis,[19] and shortly afterwards the horrific episode of the mob killing and dismemberment of American private security consultants occurred.[20] No one is sure who is behind the Sunni insurgency, and perhaps numerous organizations are committed to resistance.[21]

The Shiite uprisings that broke out in four cities in early April 2004 were, however, spearheaded by an organized militia, followers of the cleric Moktada al-Sadr, whose popular Baghdad newspaper had been shut down by American soldiers a few days earlier.[22] In the aftermath of the uprisings, al-Sadr retreated to the

Grand Mosque of al-Kufa, a city one hundred miles south of Baghdad, where his militia were effectively in control.[23] Meanwhile, huge amounts of American money have been spent with no real end in sight. "Iraq is so violent and chaotic now that it would be highly irresponsible to pull the troops out," wrote Ian Buruma, and this before the uprisings of Sunnis and Shiites that began in late March.[24] The weapons of mass destruction that were the main justification for the invasion of Iraq have not been found. Much of Iraqi infrastructure is still inadequate. Electric services have improved, but there is less drinking water than before the war, and hospitals are a disaster.[25]

To reduce its responsibility for what is becoming a quagmire—when suicide bombings killed at least 200 Shiite worshipers in March 2004, the Americans were blamed[26]—the United States, although it apparently has no intention of actually leaving Iraq,[27] is desperate to create something that will look like an Iraqi government. After a number of failed attempts, Iraqi leaders agreed to an interim constitution in March, and Shiite leaders signed only to immediately call for amendments before the charter would be implemented.[28] The Shiite leadership wants to ensure its influence in the new government will reflect the fact that Shiites are a majority of the population.[29] There are other potential problems, not least that the interim constitution recognizes all "laws, regulations, orders, and directives" issued by the U.S. occupation authorities.[30] U.S. officials are also eager to enlist the help of the United Nations in the process of setting up an Iraqi government, for fear that otherwise the new government will lack legitimacy in the eyes of ordinary Arabs, but that move is also disputed by members of the Governing Council who want a guarantee that the UN will not endorse the interim constitution.[31] Bush is determined that something resembling an Iraqi government be established by June 30, but the deadline is now in doubt.

The situation in Afghanistan is troubled as well. Warlords remain in power outside of Kabul, a renewed Taliban campaign is under way in the south, backed by al-Qaeda forces, and armed attacks on both foreign and Afghani aid workers are occurring throughout the country. The death toll has been mounting with more than 600 people killed since August 2003,[32] and the insurgents are now targeting women and children as well as aid workers. The UN has decided half the country's provinces are too dangerous for its aid workers, and most international aid agencies have fled the southern provinces. In spring 2004, the United States began a new military offensive against Taliban and al-Qaeda forces,[33] while factional fighting erupted in the western Afghan city of Herāt.[34] Nevertheless, the Bush administration, looking toward the 2004 presidential election, is determined that elections in Afghanistan go forward by June, as agreed to in the Bonn agreement of December 2001, but almost no one else, not the UN, or most European countries, or most NGOs, agrees.[35]

Meanwhile, the Israeli slaying of Hamas founder and spiritual leader Sheik Ahmed Yasmin in March 2004 set off huge protests in Gaza, Damascus, Cairo, Amman, and across the Middle East.[36] Bombings and gun battles erupted in Uzbekistan, claiming forty-seven lives.[37] And the terrorist assault on commuter trains in Madrid and the subsequent defeat of the reigning party there generated tremors across the world, not only about the fear of attacks, but about the political consequences of alliance with the United States. The South Koreans announced they would not send troops to Kirkuk as planned; the Dutch opposition Labor Party called for a July withdrawal of Dutch troops; the Polish president claimed his country had been hoodwinked; the German foreign minister announced that NATO could not consider deployment to Iraq, and so on.[38]

The lack of a clear victory in Iraq and continuing violence elsewhere, by draining some of the patriotic enthusiasm for war, opened the administration and its arguments for war to scrutiny and to doubt. Questions about Iraq's weapons of mass destruction were especially important, because the dangers posed by these weapons were so central to the administration's public argument for an invasion, and were in fact the sole justification the administration used when it sought congressional and Security Council action to justify the war.[39]

Public scrutiny was especially intense after David Kay, chief American weapons inspector in Iraq who was stepping down from his post, told Congress he was convinced Iraq had no such weapons. Kay had once been hawkish, sure that trailers found in Iraq were mobile biological facilities and sure that aluminum tubes found were evidence of the pursuit of nuclear weapons. Now he told the senators there were no WMD stockpiles, they had been destroyed during the 1990s.[40]

Administration officials sprang into action to undo the damage. George Tenet, head of intelligence, defended the pre-war judgments, and Donald Rumsfeld, secretary of defense, said it was "possible but not likely" that Iraq had no weapons at the start of the war, and he thought the weapons could still be found.[41] But the damage could not easily be undone. Secretary of State Colin L. Powell even admitted that he was not sure he would have recommended an invasion if he had known Iraq had no stockpiles of weapons.

It was as if a tightly locked Pandora's box had been pried open, and some of the contents were spilling out. The Carnegie Endowment for International Peace issued a report suggesting that pressure from the administration had led intelligence analysts to their threatening judgments about weapons of mass destruction.[42] And intelligence experts themselves began to come forward complaining about administration pressure to tailor their analyses to justify war. "Everyone knew," said Greg Thielman, a WMD specialist at the State Department's Bureau of Intelligence and Research who worked on Iraq until he retired in 2002, "that the White House was deaf to any information that would not substantiate its charges."[43] Even George Tenet explained that while the intelligence community had concluded Saddam wanted nuclear weapons, it had also made clear that as of late 2002, he had none, and probably wouldn't have any until sometime between 2007 and 2009 at the earliest.[44]

On the defensive, the administration announced it would form a commission to investigate pre-war intelligence, hoping to put the matter to rest. The president showed no haste, however. He did not announce his appointments to the commission until April 1, 2004, and the commission will not report until well after the election.[45]

Weapons of mass destruction were not the only issue surfacing to challenge the war policy. A commission already established to investigate the 9/11 attacks (the National Commission on Terrorist Attacks Upon the United States) became embroiled in conflict with the White House over the administration's refusal to give the commission access to documents or to allow officials to testify. The White House also tried to refuse the commission's request for an extension of its reporting deadline to July, no doubt for fear the findings would play a role in the election campaign.

The commission's investigation could be important because it could probe issues so far largely ignored, such as the administration's relations with the Saudis and Pakistan. Most of the 9/11 hijackers were Saudi, and the commission might well probe the relations of other Saudis, particularly Saudi clerics, with al-Qaeda.[46] Boasts of vigilance and toughness in the war on terror might not stand up in an accounting of the administration's haste in airlifting Saudi nationals, including members of the bin Laden family, out of the country within days of the 9/11 attacks, when private air travel was banned. And then there is the close relationship the administration has developed with Pakistan, an ostensible ally and the recipient of substantial American aid whose government was almost certainly implicated in large-scale shipments of nuclear material and technology to Iran, Libya, North Korea, and other hostile states.[47]

By March 2004, the administration was ready to compromise on the 9/11 investigation and agreed to extend the commission's deadline. The president, it was announced, would appear before the commission for one hour (at which John Kerry shot back, "If the President of the United States can find time to go to a rodeo," referring to a Houston rodeo Bush had attended, "he can find time to do more than an hour in front of a commission that is investigating what happened to America's intelligence.")[48]

The hearings turned out to be surprising and explosive. Richard A. Clarke, counter-terrorism coordinator under the Reagan, Clinton, and both Bush presidencies, charged that the Bush administration ignored repeated warnings because they were so intent on attacking Iraq.[49] He began his testimony with an appeal to the families of the 9/11 victims whose persistent lobbying led to the hearings.[50] "Your government failed you," he said. "Those entrusted with protecting you failed you. And I failed you. We tried hard, but that doesn't matter, because we failed. And for that failure, I would ask, once all the facts are out, for your understanding and forgiveness."[51]

The cascading revelations inspired others to speak out.[52] Former Secretary of the Navy James Webb made one of the stronger statements: "Bush arguably has committed the greatest strategic blunder in modern memory. To put it bluntly, he attacked the wrong target. . . . There is no historical precedent for taking such action when our country was not being directly threatened. The reckless course that Bush and his advisers have set will affect the economic and military energy of our nation for decades."[53] As the new charges, and the administration's countercharges[54] (which consisted mainly of accusing Clark of making his claims in order to sell his book) kept bubbling up in the press, the White House finally agreed on March 29 to allow Condoleezza Rice to testify under oath.[55] Only a day or so later, the commission announced it was pressing the White House to explain why the administration blocked thousands of pages of Clinton-era documents from being turned over to the panel's investigators.[56] On April 2, the administration agreed to turn over the documents.[57] Even before Rice testified, the *New York Times* had pieced together an account summed up by the headline: "Halting Response Seen to Terror Risk in Summer '01."[58]

Meanwhile, inquiries about the president's service in the Vietnam War were making the front pages, precipitated when moviemaker Michael Moore called the president a "deserter," and Terry McAuliffe, head of the Democratic National Committee, chimed in that Bush had been "AWOL." The president then found himself defending his record as a National Guard recruit during the Vietnam War and, indeed, even defending the fact that he had somehow managed to get into the National Guard at a time when regular army troops were the ones being sent to Vietnam.

And then there was the ongoing federal grand jury investigation to determine who in the White House disclosed the identity of Valerie Plame, an undercover CIA agent and the wife of former Ambassador Joseph Wilson. Wilson had traveled to Africa in February 2002 at the request of the CIA and found no evidence to support the administration's claim that Niger had supplied raw uranium to Iraq in the 1980s. He published this conclusion in the *New York Times* on July 6, 2003. Someone among the angry

White House officials disclosed Plame's identity, apparently in revenge. The ensuing FBI investigation spread through much of the White House, and included Karl Rove, the president's senior political advisor, and I. Lewis Libby, the vice president's chief of staff.[59] Then, in a seemingly minor matter, a House subcommittee hearing disclosed that the White House had spurned an FBI request for a mere $12 million to hire eighty more investigators to track and disrupt global financial networks that support terrorist groups.[60]

Multiple accusations were also surfacing against Halliburton. The Justice Department was investigating a consortium that included Halliburton subsidiary Kellogg, Brown & Root for allegedly illegal payments in connection with the construction of a natural gas plant in Nigeria in the late 1990s when Cheney was chief executive officer.[61] The Pentagon was holding back payments to Halliburton because of what it called "substantial" overcharges on its generous Iraq contracts.[62] As scandals multiplied, some in the press and the Congress even began to question their own role in accepting the administration's misleading information. "The press did not do their job," concluded Michael Massing in the *New York Review of Books*. And Democrats in the Congress made lists, reporting 237 specific misleading statements by the five administration officials most responsible for providing public information.[63]

These multiplying investigations and the questions they raised about the legitimacy of the Bush war policy, and indeed the legitimacy of Bush himself, would be unlikely if the patriotic enthusiasm of the nation were not already fading. But the revelations in turn also contribute to the growing sense of the ambiguities of the war. In any case, historical experience argues that the populations of states at war are not so easily and cheaply hoodwinked as Göring thought, or at least not for long. True, people tend to rally behind their leaders in the face of foreign threats, real or fabricated. But the rush of support generated by war rarely lasts long. Only recall that the Gulf War drove the approval ratings of the first President Bush to astronomical levels as the country bedecked itself with yellow ribbons to honor our troops. Six months later, the president's poll ratings were plummeting, and shortly after that he was defeated for reelection.

Modern warfare requires the participation of the population, their willingness to serve in the field of battle, to submit to "confiscatory taxation, and allow the conversion of productive capacities to the ends of war," writes Charles Tilly in a study of war-making in European states. However, as war and the sacrifice it demands grinds on, patriotic enthusiasms ebb, and popular resistance rises: "Although a call to defend the fatherland stimulated extraordinary support for the efforts of war . . . war made any state vulnerable to popular resistance, and answerable to popular demands, as never before."[64] And American presidents turned commanders-in-chief during extended wars seemed to recognize their debt to the civilian population. In the 1960s, Lyndon Baines Johnson was desperate to maintain the policies that provided both "guns and butter." As a consequence, escalating spending on the military was accompanied by escalating spending on social programs. Eventually, of course, even guns and butter were not sufficient to sustain popular support for a remote and murderous war without end. Flagging troop morale and flagging public support combined to produce the huge defeat of forced American withdrawal, and to create the "Vietnam syndrome" of fear of military entanglements that this administration is said to have been determined to overcome.

In other words, history suggests that war-making, as it continues, has required governments to strike bargains with their people, to make concessions. Wars "give a powerful momentum to already existing pro-democratic pressures."[65] In the past, these concessions have taken the form of enlarged popular political rights, and expanded government efforts to improve the economic well-being of important popular sectors. The history of other countries provides striking examples of this sort of wartime bargain. Göran Therborn in a careful study of the history of the franchise and electoral-representative institutions, concludes that democratic arrangements spread after the First World War when the number of democracies increased from three to ten, and the number of countries that at least gave the vote to males increased from five to fourteen. "The big boom of democracy," however, "came in the aftermath of the Second World War, with only Swiss sexism and U.S. racism holding out until the 1970s. The conclusion would appear to be that bourgeois democracy is largely a martial accomplishment."[66]

A similar pattern seems to hold for state policies that shore up the income of ordinary people. Bismarck, who introduced the first national health and pension systems in Europe, was also the great state builder and war-maker. The initial German programs, like the programs that followed elsewhere in Europe, were small, reaching only minorities of the population. But in the immediate aftermath of World War II most European countries greatly expanded their social welfare programs. In England this expansion had been prefigured by the 1943 White Paper, authored by William Beveridge in the midst of war, promising the British people a greatly expanded welfare state once the war ended. Tilly concludes: "From the nineteenth century to the recent past . . . all European states involved themselves much more heavily than before in building social infrastructure, providing services, in regulating economic activity, in controlling population movements, and in assuring citizens' welfare; all these activities began as products of rulers' efforts to acquire revenues and compliance from the subject populations, but took on lives and rationales of their own."[67]

American history reveals a similar pattern of tacit bargaining with a population forced to bear the costs of war. To be sure, wars or the threat of wars have also spurred repressive measures, justified by the war emergency. The Alien and Sedition Acts were passed when war with France threatened. When the United States entered World War I, the Espionage Act of 1917 and the Sedition Act of 1918 led to the jailing of leaders of the International Workers of the World. Japanese Americans were rounded up and placed in internment camps in World War II.

But the repression of particular groups was typically accompanied or followed by major concessions to the larger population in the form of expanded democratic rights and social welfare measures. Laura Jensen reports on the commitments of the Continental Congress to provide for men injured in the Revolutionary War, and to give land to certain classes of veterans both of the Revolutionary War and the War of 1812.[68] After the Civil War, pensions were granted to war veterans and their families, and the Thirteenth, Fourteenth, and Fifteenth amendments extended citizenship and voting rights to the freed slaves, many of whom had fought with the Union Army and had helped reverse the tide of battle. World War I saw the repression of some of the most radical labor leaders, but it also led President Woodrow Wilson to announce support for collective bargaining rights for labor unions.

Similarly, during World War II, the federal government incarcerated Japanese Americans and extracted no-strike pledges from most unions, but it also conciliated the unions with the War Labor Board's maintenance of membership policies that enlarged union membership and treasuries. And after the war, a system of exceedingly generous veterans' benefits was introduced. As the national debate on civil rights began in 1946, Senator Alben Barkley of

Kentucky pointed to the relationship between wartime exactions and citizen rights: "I voted, Mr. President, to extend the arm of the federal government into every home and into every city and into every town in the United States and take from the homes and communities every able-bodied man available for military service without regard to race, color, creed, religion, ancestry or origin. . . . I do not see how I, having voted to subject men to compulsory service in behalf of our institutions in wartime, can refuse to vote for the same kind of democracy in peace when the war has been won."[69] During the Vietnam War the federal government finally moved to enforce the rights first granted the freed slaves after the Civil War, social welfare programs were expanded, new national health programs were introduced in the form of Medicaid and Medicare, and the right to vote was extended to the eighteen-year-olds who were fighting in southeast Asia.

True, not all of these concessions endured. Civil War pensions atrophied as the veterans died off, southern states successfully countermanded the rights granted the freed slaves under the federal constitution, Woodrow Wilson's support of collective bargaining rights did not have much practical consequence. Nevertheless, the regularity of the pattern suggests a powerful underlying dynamic of reciprocal bargaining in the relation of governments at war to their populations.

What about now? "There are internal reasons" writes Eric Hobsbawm "why the American empire may not last, the most immediate being that most Americans are not interested in imperialism or world domination in the sense of running the world. What they are interested in is what happens to them in the U.S."[70] Are there signs, then, that the Bush administration realizes the centrality of domestic issues and is moving to honor the historic bargain, to compensate the ordinary Americans who are paying for war?

6

REGIME CHANGE?

A GOOD PLACE to look for evidence of the regime's efforts to placate potential popular discontent is the 2004 campaign for the presidency. The president's political operatives are certainly not unaware of the need to appeal to Americans by claiming to have taken major steps to improve their well-being. Bush is championed not only as the war president, but as the education president who gave us the No Child Left Behind Act, thus breaking with the decades-long Republican opposition to a strong federal role in education. Reagan had actually vowed to eliminate the federal Department of Education. Underlying this position was the Republican animosity toward the teacher unions, who have been staunch backers of the Democrats. Bush's reversal of the usual Republican stance toward a federal role in education was key to his claims to "compassionate conservatism."

But the implementation of the No Child Left Behind requirements regarding pupil testing, penalties to school districts for educational failure, and teacher qualifications has aroused furor on all sides, including in staunchly Republican states.[1] In Oklahoma, legislators passed a resolution calling on Congress to repeal the act, and received a standing ovation. In Virginia, the Republican-controlled House of Delegates passed a resolution, 98 to 1, urging Congress to exempt Virginia from the law. In Pennsylvania, 138 school superintendents protested provisions of the law. The Republican-controlled Utah House prohibited state authorities from spending money to implement the law. Legislative chambers in twelve states have taken actions of this sort, usually with the support of both Democrats and states-rights Republicans. And fourteen states have asked the Bush administration to revise the education law in order to allow them to use their own methods for measuring academic gains.[2] More generous federal funding of the law would help keep these protests at bay. But of course, higher outlays for education in the wake of big tax cuts and rising military spending would provoke an outcry from an increasingly deficit-conscious Congress. As a result, the law has been funded less generously than promised, and other education funds have actually been cut,[3] contributing to spreading conflicts where Bush had expected to garner support.

The president's campaign boasts that he honored his promise in 2000 to give seniors subsidized prescription drugs with the Medicare expansion signed into law in December 2003. Karl Rove, who understands the importance of domestic issues in the 2004 election, purportedly decided this should be a main focus of the campaign fully eighteen months before the election.[4] In fact, the drug benefits offered seniors under the Medicare Prescription Drug Act are patchy and limited, and tempered by provisions that prevent the importation of lower cost drugs from Canada, and also forbid the government from negotiating for lower drug prices. But since the legislation is not to take effect until well after the election, the administration's spin about its achievement will not be shadowed by the disappointment of actual experiences with the plan. Other events, however, have intervened. One is the considerable indignation over the tactics used to pass the legislation. The House is conducting an ethics investigation into charges of bribery by Representative Nick Smith who says he was offered $100,000 for his son's congressional campaign in return for his vote. Smith's allegations also led the press to pay more attention to the "unprecedented and outrageous extension of the vote for nearly three hours" while arms were twisted to get the needed votes.[5]

Then there was the news that the General Accounting Office, an investigative arm of the Congress, was looking into advertisements and brochures prepared by the Bush administration to publicize the new Medicare law. Actors posed as journalists, making the videos appear to be newscasts, and both the brochures and videos are, said the general counsel of the accounting office, flawed by "omissions and other weaknesses." This appears to be a cautious understatement since the videos were clearly hype, advertisements cast as news so that local television programs would rebroadcast them. One included pictures of the president receiving a standing ovation from a crowd as he signed the law, while an actor hired as narrator intones, "In Washington, I'm Karen Ryan reporting." Documents from the Medicare agency show that something on the order of $50 million was budgeted for this advertising in the year leading up to the election.[6]

Another outcry erupted after the White House itself acknowledged that its cost estimates for the Medicare expansion had been too low. Richard S. Foster, a Medicare actuary, said he had been threatened with being fired if he shared with Congress his estimates of the cost of the legislation, which were substantially higher than the White House was claiming at the time.[7] Democrats in Congress demanded an investigation of this as well, and the House Ways and Means Committee held hearings in spring 2004.[8] And in its annual report to Congress, the Medicare board of trustees reported that the trust fund could run out of money by the end of the decade.[9] Together, the scandals have cast a shadow on administration claims about Medicare prescription drugs as a benefit for the elderly. A sign of the shifting tides on Medicare was the statement of Senator Trent Lott, former Republican Senate leader, that he would support legislation to allow importation of low-cost prescription drugs, which the Medicare law prohibits. "I cannot explain to my mother any longer" the senator said, "why she should pay twice or two-thirds more than what is paid in Canada and Mexico."[10]

The president is in a close race, and immigrant voters could make the difference. Accordingly, the campaign also advertises the Bush proposal to allow a limited legalization for undocumented immigrants as a gain for immigrants, especially Mexican Americans who are important in some of the battleground states. Because it is presented as a step toward legalization, which immigrants desperately want, the proposal has sown some confusion in the immigrant community. Most immigrant advocacy and labor groups seem deeply skeptical, however. In any case, for the time being, the administration's proposal is stalled, largely because of opposition from conservative Republicans who object to any kind of amnesty for undocumented workers.[11]

Arab Americans are another immigrant group important to the election. Most of them supported Bush in 2000, and they may be key to victory in the battleground states of Florida, Michigan, Ohio, and Pennsylvania. But they have turned against the administration. A Zogby poll shows that Arab Americans now strongly disapprove of Bush, preferring Kerry by 78 percent to 12 percent. The most contentious issue among these voters is Bush's support of Israel's prime minister, Ariel Sharon. "Another sore spot is the administration's crackdown on Arab immigrants, especially following the September 11 terrorist attacks. 'There is a feeling that our community is being scapegoated and our civil rights are being violated,' says Taleb Salhab, coordinator of the Arab American Leadership Council in Florida."[12] Arab Americans are, not surprisingly, the main targets of the civil rights restrictions that followed the passage of the Patriot Act.

By spring 2004, jobs and the economy had displaced the war in

Iraq or terrorism as top voter concerns.[13] The administration responded by boasting of its economic recovery program, meaning mainly the tax cuts, both those that had already been legislated, and the additional cuts Bush intends to push through Congress. In February 2004 as the presidential campaign began, Bush released a report claiming his economic plan would create 2.6 million new jobs.[14] In February 2003 the administration had predicted its policies would create 1.7 million new jobs.[15] In October 2003, Treasury Secretary John W. Snow predicted 200,000 new jobs a month for the following twelve months. And before that, the administration predicted the creation of 5.5 million jobs between July 2003 and the end of 2004.[16] In fact, the economy has not added enough jobs to keep up with the growth of the workforce, and the administration now distances itself from all these claims.[17]

But this did not change the administration's tune. "Higher taxes right now," said Bush in a March 2004 campaign swing in Orlando, Florida, "would undermine growth and destroy jobs just as our economy is getting stronger."[18] But legislative titles notwithstanding, the tax cuts have produced few jobs.[19] True, there has been an economic upturn, profits are soaring, and employment is beginning to expand as well, to the relief of the White House. But overall the Bush administration has presided over the loss of more than 2 to 3 million jobs, largely because corporations are squeezing productivity gains out of their existing workforces. True, the March reports did show a surge in job creation of 308,000 jobs.[20] If the turnaround continues, the administration will have a much stronger hand going into the election.

But if it doesn't, then this will be the first time since 1939 that the number of jobs has not recovered to pre-recession levels nearly three years after the onset of the recession.[21] Moreover, the tax cuts may even be implicated in part of the job loss. Todd Buchholz, a former White House economic advisor under the first President Bush commented, "If you were a manager, why would you hire a human being instead of a machine? Humans get sick. They daydream. And they take coffee breaks."[22] Changes in the tax code that reduced taxes on most dividends and capital gains and increased the write-offs that are permitted businesses for new equipment purchases, make it cheaper for employers to substitute equipment for people.[23]

Technological innovation is a long-term trend, although it is encouraged by the Bush tax cuts. It may not be as important to job loss as overwork and speedup, which have accelerated under the Bush administration.[24] James K. Galbraith argues that downsizing firms do not so much increase productivity through technological innovation as they squeeze wages.[25] Outsourcing is also a factor in the loss of jobs, and the Bush administration has aggressively promoted trade accords.[26] This too is a political sore spot. When N. Gregory Mankiw, the chair of the president's Council of Economic Advisers, remarked that sending high-tech jobs abroad is "probably a plus" for the U.S. economy over the long term, he set off a small storm, forcing Republican leaders to suddenly pretend they were ardent protectionists.[27] A survey by the *Financial Times* of the one hundred largest American companies shows they paid 30.6 percent of their 2003 income in taxes, down from 33 percent the previous year, which the *Times* attributes to the growing share of their activity taking place overseas.[28]

Whether the cause for job loss is increased productivity or squeezed workers or outsourcing—and all of these reasons are part of the story[29]—unemployment remains high for a recovery, and many of the unemployed appear to be giving up the search for work, which means they are no longer counted as unemployed. Manufacturing, where workers are unionized and better paid, has been especially hard hit. The industry that added the most workers is temporary help, followed by health care and restaurant work, which are less likely to be unionized, and where the pay is low.[30] In New York City, nearly half of black men between the ages of sixteen and sixty-four were jobless, according to federal Bureau of Employment Statistics data analyzed by Mark Levitan of the Community Service Society. Bob Herbert reported that when Local 46 of the Metallic Lathers Union announced that it would allow 200 people to apply for membership, which meant a shot at high-paying work, the line of applicants circled the block. Early arrivals waited in line for three days.[31] Meanwhile, the administration came under fire for proposing as its new "manufacturing czar" Anthony Raimondo, who as the CEO of a manufacturing company in Nebraska had outsourced 75 of his own workers and built a $3 million factory in China to employ 165 Chinese workers.[32]

Wages are lagging along with job creation, and this may emerge as the bigger problem for the Bush campaign, provided that the Democrats are not too intimidated by charges of "class warfare" to push the issue. "At this point in a normal recovery, total real labor compensation would be up by about 2.6 percent," writes Laura D'Andrea Tyson, dean of the London Business School. "Instead, it is down by more than 3 percent. As a result of anemic job and wage growth, America's consumers are missing about $350 billion to $400 billion in income, compared to past cycles."[33]

Soaring profits and stagnant wages mean, of course, that inequality, already at peak levels when the Bush administration took office, is growing.[34] "What is happening," says Bob Herbert, is nothing short of historic. The American workers' share of the increase in national income since November 2001, the end of the last recession, is the lowest on record. Employers took the money and ran."[35] Profits never stopped rising as a share of national income during the recent recession,[36] and the median pay of chief executives also continued to rise, albeit at a much slower rate than during the boom years of the 1990s.[37] Now during the economic recovery, profits are soaring, but wages are stagnating, consumer debt is skyrocketing at an annual rate of 11.5 percent as the costs of such basics as housing, health insurance, and transportation increase but wages do not.[38] Consistent with these trends, poverty is increasing; last year another 1.7 million Americans slipped below the poverty line.[39] The U.S. Conference of Mayors reports growing homelessness and hunger, with most of the cities surveyed reporting they had been forced to turn away people requesting help.[40] And after more than two decades of shying away from the poverty issue for fear of Republican scorn, the Democratic contenders for the presidential nomination began to talk about poverty, calling for a higher minimum wage, job-generating public works, subsidized college tuition in exchange for community service, and the re-legalization of a worker's right to join a union.[41]

Normally, Republican administrations become economic populists as presidential elections approach. Both Ronald Reagan and Richard Nixon ran with economic growth strong and unemployment low. Nixon even imposed price-wage controls which, says James K. Galbraith, "drove real wages through the roof."[42] With the costs of war rising, and the legitimacy of war collapsing, economic populism would seem to be more necessary than ever. "I'm against everything this president has done, said an unemployed pipefitter and electrician from Phoenix who carried a sign that said: "Read My Lips: No New Jobs" in the New York City march to commemorate the first anniversary of the invasion of Iraq.[43] But there isn't actually much the administration can do about the weakness of its popular economic appeals without weakening its main domestic agenda.

The Bush economic stimulus plan consists of sharply increased military spending and big tax cuts for business and the affluent. This sort of deficit spending is a variant of Keynesianism that "has particular appeal for Republicans. Instead of growing the government in general—pumping resources into public works, health care and education, say, which would have an immediate knock-on effect on sorely needed job creation—the policy focuses on those areas that represent obvious conservative and business-friendly constituencies. . . . that tend to be big contributors to Republican Party funds."[44] James K. Galbraith thinks that "economic stagnation is to their taste. They don't want a new recession, obviously, and they look set to avoid that. But do they really want full employment and strong labor unions and rising wages? Probably not. The oil, mining, defense, media, and pharmaceutical firms who form the core of their constituency rely on monopoly power, patents, and the control of public resources for their profits. They do not depend, very much, on strong consumer demand."[45]

The administration thus has an election year dilemma. With unemployment relatively high and wages lagging, it should at least be proposing measures to protect workers who are paying the price for free trade, technological change, and lean production. But the tax cuts and military spending increases have generated a huge increase in the deficit, an increase aggravated by the administration's Medicare and education spending initiatives. A conservative backlash is brewing, encouraged by such authorities as Alan Greenspan, who urged Congress to trim future benefits "sooner rather than later."[46] Harvard's Robert Barro criticized both the tax and spending policies of the Bush administration.[47] Brian Riedl of the Heritage Foundation charges that "Reelection has become the focus of Republicans in the White House and Congress. And those in power have determined the road to staying in power is paved with government spending."[48]

To ward off those charges, Bush has repeatedly promised to freeze domestic spending increases.[49] In March, the conflict worsened as the Senate voted to approve a budget resolution that could endanger Bush's drive to make all his tax cuts permanent by requiring that new tax cuts be offset by tax increases or spending cuts. Only desperate arm-twisting by Republican leaders prevented the adoption of a similar plan in the House.[50] For most Republicans, the problem was spending. Representative Jeb Hensarling, freshman Republican from Texas, said "I didn't come to Congress to grow the government."[51]

The opposition provoked by soaring deficits, in turn, inhibits the administration from even offering the usual palliatives for job and wage loss. True, as election 2004 approached, the president asked Congress for a $500 million job-training appropriation for the fiscal year 2005,[52] but he also proposed eliminating cash assistance for workers displaced by the North American Free Trade Agreement, and Congress stalled on the extension of long-term unemployment insurance. By April, the president had shifted ground, announcing a doubling of the number of workers in training, to be achieved by administrative changes and without any new funds.[53] The president's proposals took no account of the reductions Congress had already enacted of $800,000 or 12 percent since 2001.[54] Similarly, in a radio address in March, the president said he had asked Congress for $200 million more this year to support home ownership through the American Dream Down Payment home ownership program, and did not mention that he had also asked for cuts of $1.6 billion in housing vouchers.[55]

Meanwhile, the welfare rolls continued to shrink as a result of changes in the program introduced in 1996 when Clinton struck a devil's deal with congressional Republicans. Wade Horn, assistant secretary of Health and Human Services in charge of welfare policy commented that the welfare program had become relatively "recession proof," and he was right. The application process had become so torturous, and the program so humiliating and punitive, that it could no longer function as the ultimate recourse for the unemployed and impoverished.[56] In March 2004, a bill was before the Senate to renew the welfare law, albeit with stricter work requirements and a program to promote "healthy marriages" touted by the president. When a bipartisan Senate majority voted to include increased funds for child care in the bill to take account of the increased work requirements, the administration objected vigorously.[57] When the Democrats tried to attach an amendment to preserve overtime pay for several million white-collar workers, the majority leader used a parliamentary maneuver to avoid a vote. Then a Democratic effort to attach an amendment to increase the minimum wage, from $5.15 to $7 an hour, resulted in the defeat of the entire bill.[58]

Other means-tested programs had also been affected by the 1996 law. New York City reported that as of September 2003, a half million fewer people were participating in the food stamp program than at the time of the adoption of the law.[59] And nationally, what the federal government calls "food insecurity," has been rising.[60] The *Economist,* commenting on Bush's State of the Union in January, said he "gave a speech that was almost Clintonian in its small-bore obsessions."[61] No wonder. There wasn't much he could propose without undermining his main agenda or aggravating the deficit issue.

Campaign sloganeering aside, the administration seems to be in a tight spot. David Brooks says "plans are in the works" for a "comprehensive domestic policy vision." No doubt Brooks hopes so. But so far, the Bush regime initiatives are so deeply constrained and compromised by its main business-oriented policy agenda that the domestic initiatives it parades to show it is concerned with the well-being of ordinary Americans cannot stand up to scrutiny. This is not the result of missteps or miscalculations or simple oversight. A business-oriented administration gave us business-oriented policies that strip away environmental and other regulatory protections, cut back social welfare programs or turn them into opportunities for private profit, and slash taxes on corporations and the better off. All this was at the very heart of the Republican business agenda, the raison d'être for its scramble for domestic power, a scramble which the fear of terrorism and the excitement of war promoted and obscured, at least for a time. The White House makes claims about championing the well-being of Americans, and dresses those claims in slogans. But its policies have in fact violated the historic bargain that war-making governments have made with their people. War itself cannot be an effective cover for this ruse for long. The costs and ambiguities of continuing war, and the debilitating scandals that war has provoked, are likely to increase popular discontent over the failure of the administration to honor its professed responsibility for the well-being of its own population.

But will disillusion over Iraq and popular dissatisfaction with domestic policies defeat the administration? Much could intervene. No one knows how the military situation in Iraq and Afghanistan will develop, and no one can be sure either of whether there will be continuing revelations here at home. "It is hard to remember," writes Adam Nagourney, "a presidential campaign with so many potentially critical and unpredictable events on the horizon, poised to rewrite the story line of the race within a news cycle."

And then there is the question of how events are interpreted by the media. Until very recently, the Bush White House was successful in getting the media to accept its version of the truth. It was only in the wake of a cascade of leaks and denunciations by insiders that the press began to question the administration's claims about the reasons for war, or about its preparedness in dealing with terrorist attacks. Until the photos of torture at Abu Ghraib were revealed, the press continued to be reluctant to publish the images of death in Iraq that helped build opposition to the war in Vietnam.[62]

It is not only that the big media corporations are allied with the Bush regime. It is also that individual newspeople cower before the aggressiveness of the administration. After 9/11, Dan Rather said on the David Letterman Show that "I would willingly die for my country at a moment's notice and on the command of my president." A year later, as a guest on BBC's Newsnight, he explained: "In some ways, the fear is that you will be necklaced here, you will have a flaming tire of lack of patriotism put around your neck. It's that fear that keeps journalists from asking the toughest of the tough questions."[63]

His vulnerabilities on Iraq and domestic policy notwithstanding, Bush could well win the election. The Republicans have already made clear that they will campaign on national security, which means they will try to reawaken the fear and euphoria associated with war. They may even arrange events so that a new war occurs in time for the election. One suspects, indeed, that the electoral calculations of Karl Rove, the administration's Machiavelli, had a good deal to do with the timing and conduct of the invasion first in Afghanistan and then in Iraq. The invasion clearly helped the Republicans in the midterm election, and they hope to call up memories of 9/11 by holding the Republican convention in New York City. The apparatus now in place to collect bits of information on terrorism from around the world increases the likelihood of reports of new and alarming terrorist threats, even barring the possibility of a more devious conspiracy to actually create such threats.

And then there is the possibility of a new "October surprise" in the form, one can speculate, of an announcement that Usama bin Laden is now in the hands of the Pakistani or American authorities. When the capture of Saddam Hussein was announced in December 2003, Bush's approval ratings jumped six points, and his reelection prospects brightened.[64] Or perhaps the election will be conducted while the spectacle of a trial of Saddam Hussein is underway.[65]

It is already clear that the administration will invoke the right-wing agenda of sex and guns in the campaign to activate the ranks of the populist right. On April 1 the president signed the Unborn Victims of Violence Act which makes it a crime to harm a fetus.[66] While the law exempts legally performed abortions, it establishes definitions that are dangerous for abortion rights by defining a "child in utero" as "a member of the species homo sapiens at any stage of development, who is carried in the womb." This is clearly another step in the long and ongoing battle against abortion rights which the Justice Department is also pursuing by trying to force hospitals and clinics to turn over medical records on thousands of abortions.[67] The sex issues play well to the right-wing base, and the growing uproar over gay marriage is a gift to the White House for it allows the president to campaign on his support for a constitutional amendment defining marriage as the joining of a man and a woman. Then, in a stunning move, the White House dropped even the pretense of supporting gun control measures,[68] in deference we can be sure to the National Rifle Association and its far-flung constituency of gun owners.

If all else fails, the multiple manipulations of the vote and the vote count that occurred in Florida in the 2000 election could re-

cur, perhaps on a larger scale and with the aid of electronic voting
machines. One of the scandalous elements in the Florida 2000
election was that secretary of state Katherine Harris, the chief
state election official, was also the cochair of the Florida
Bush–Cheney campaign. Among other things, Harris used her authority as secretary of state to preside over the disenfranchisement
of thousands of African Americans on the grounds that they were
released felons, a process that it turned out disenfranchised many
non-felons as well. Now Republican secretaries of states in Missouri and Michigan, both battleground states, have also taken top
positions in the Bush–Cheney campaign.

One of the outcomes of the Florida scandal was the passage of
a law called the Help America Vote Act (HAVA) which was supposed to avoid future debacles by modernizing state election procedures. The law also introduced new and confusing requirements
for voter identification, which are certain to be even more confusing when they are implemented by the states and counties. They
can also be implemented in ways that disenfranchise many voters,
especially less-educated voters. And then there are the electronic
voting machines that HAVA helped the states pay for. The executive of the largest of the companies making these machines is an
outspoken Republican activist. No one knows whether the machines already in use were fixed to corrupt past vote counts, particularly in the 2002 midterm elections. But computer scientists
are clear that fixing the machines to fix an election would be child's
play. "I've been watching all the elements fall into place for two
possible political catastrophes," says John W. Dean in his new
book, *Worse than Watergate*, "one that will take the air out of the
Bush–Cheney balloon and the other, far more disquieting, that
will take the air out of democracy."[69]

Still, the air could go out of the balloon and Bush could lose.
For one thing, Iraq has turned into a quagmire. "A year to the day

after going to war to topple Saddam Hussein, President George Bush is weaker at home, widely disliked abroad, and struggling to hold together the fraying 'coalition of the willing' that now occupies Iraq. To a large extent, Mr. Bush's electoral prospects are now prisoner of what happens in Iraq."[70] Moreover, the lift in public approval that wars generate rarely lasts very long under any circumstances. The president's father hit a peak of 89 percent approval in a Gallup poll conducted in early March 1991 just after the Gulf War ended. In a few months his rating reverted to the mid-60 percent range, where they had been before the gulf crisis began. The boost presidents get in public support in response to foreign crises are usually short-lived.[71]

All of which argues that in a closely divided electorate, the Democrats have a shot at the presidency. There can be no question but that defeating Bush would be a good thing, for the country, and the world. To be sure, a Kerry administration would also pursue American imperial interests, not least our interest in oil. Nevertheless it would temper American military aggression, work to restore multilateral relations, and to restore a role for the UN, although it would not, indeed could not, pull our troops out of Iraq. We are probably fated to remain there for a long time.

Kerry's domestic policies would be more tempered as well. He would surely work to modify the tax cuts, and since he is not tied to the energy industry, he would also try to restore a framework of environmental regulation. But left to its own designs, a Kerry administration's policies would be timid and hedged in. It would be mindful of the empire of bases and the interests entangled in them; it would be limited on the home front by the tax cuts it could not modify, and also by its own effort to cultivate relations with business, and by the fact that it would likely come to office with a Republican Congress. All that acknowledged, a Kerry administration would extend our time horizons, we would survive and so would many people across the globe, making it possible to fight on other days.

Moreover, a Democratic White House would create a political context that would be far more encouraging to oppositional movements from the left. This is not simply because its rhetoric and its program would be more closely aligned with the goals of social movements. It is also because left movements can threaten a Democratic administration. Movements stage dramatic actions, and their protests can throw sand in the gears of social institutions. In these ways, they force polarizing issues onto the political agenda that are otherwise ignored, issues that risk fragmenting the reigning coalition unless they are addressed. This is why right-wing movements flourish under right-wing administrations, and why movements from the left are more likely to surge when liberal Democrats are in power. Note that I am not arguing that left movements always flourish under Democrats. Rather, my argument is that they cannot flourish without Democrats in power, a lesson imprinted in the experience of the New Deal and the 1960s. Because a Kerry administration would offer hope, especially the hope of real influence, it would be more likely to energize protests by environmentalists, or antiwar groups, or minorities, or workers, or the poor.

There is another issue, more important than tax or environmental or social policy. It is often said that lurking behind the decision of the Bush–Cheney–Rumsfeld team to invade Afghanistan and Iraq was their determination to score a victory that would demonstrate our military prowess, not only to the world at large, but to Americans as well. They would purge, once and for all, the so-called Vietnam syndrome, which the invasions of tiny Grenada and Panama had not obviously succeeded in doing. But the syndrome marks a degree of sanity in American culture, acquired at great cost to us and far greater cost to South Asia during the long war in Vietnam. The quagmire now in Iraq together with rising discontent over domestic policies could well revive the syndrome. That would be a very good thing. It would mean that the American regime could no longer mobilize the American public for costly wars in far-off places for unclear goals.

That would be a transformation well worth working for.

The political moment is thus not without hope. My main point, however, is that it is dangerous. The United States is in the grip of a ruling group that is brash, shortsighted, and greedy. There are no promises for our political future. But of course, there are never any promises, yet predatory rulers are sometimes curbed, and even defeated.

NOTES

CHAPTER 1

1. Ruy Teixeira, "Public Opinion Watch," *Century Foundation,* March 24–30, 2003.
2. Robert Borosage, "Sacrifice Is for Suckers," *Nation,* April 28, 2003.
3. Quoted in "The Budget Fight Is Now," *New York Times,* Editorial, April 3, 2003.
4. Jeffrey Gettleman, "Mix of Pride and Shame Follows Killings and Mutilation by Iraqis," *New York Times,* April 2, 2004.
5. Vali Nasr, "Iraq's Real Holy War," *New York Times,* March 6, 2004. See also John F. Burns, "The Road Ahead May Be Even Rougher," *New York Times*, March 7, 2004.
6. Arundhati Roy lists these recent American wars: Korea, Guatemala; Cuba, Laos, Cambodia, Vietnam, Grenada, Libya, El Salvador, Nicaragua, Panama, Iraq, Somalia, Sudan, Yugoslavia, and Afghanistan. See the foreword to Noam Chomsky's *For Reasons of State*, The New Press, 2003, xiii.
7. Tom Engelhardt, "Twenty-first Century Gunboat Diplomacy," Tomeditor@aol.com, March 30, 2004.
8. The most authoritative—and scathing—of these reports, issued by the Carnegie Endowment for International Peace, was written by Joseph Cirincione, George Perkovich, and the Endowment's president, Jessica Tuchman Mathews, http://www.ceip.org/files/Publications/IraqSummary.asp?

from=pubdate. In early January, the Bush administration quietly withdrew their 400-person weapon-hunting team from Iraq.

9. See Davod Rohde, "U.S. Will Celebrate Pakistan as a 'Major Non-NATO Ally,'" *New York Times,* March 19, 2004. The federal government has quietly acknowledged the renewed nuclear threat by reviving its capacity to study nuclear fallout in order to trace the sources of a nuclear event. See William J. Broad, "Addressing the Unthinkable: U.S. Revives Study of Fallout," *New York Times,* March 19, 2004.

10. See William J. Broad, "Addressing the Unthinkable: U.S. Revives Study of Fallout," *New York Times,* March 19, 2004.

11. Chalmers Johnson, "America's Empire of Bases," http://www.americanempireproject.com/.

12. See Elaine Sciolino, "Investigators See Link Involving Qaeda Cell," and David E. Sanger, "Blow to Bush: Ally Rejected," both in *New York Times,* March 15, 2004. Dennis Hastert, the speaker of the House, responded to these events by saying the Spanish people "had a huge terrorist attack within their country and they chose to change their government and to, in a sense, appease terrorists." Cited by Paul Krugman; "Taken for a Ride," *New York Times,* March 19, 2004.

13. Quoted in Noam Chomsky, "Selective Memory and a Dishonest Doctrine," *Toronto Star,* December 21, 2003.

14. See Anatol Lieven, "The Push for War," *London Review of Books,* http://www.lrb.co.uk/v24/n19/liev01_.html.

15. See for example Lutz Kleveman, "Oil and the New 'Great Game,'" *Nation,* February 16, 2004. Kleveman sees American aggression as a contest over oil and gas reserves, particularly of the Caspian region, and a rerun of the nineteenth century rivalry between Great Britain and Imperial Russia.

16. Heather Timmons, "Oil Majors Agree to Develop Big Kazakh Field," *New York Times,* February 26, 2004.

17. See Jeff Gerth, "Forecast of Rising Oil Demand Challenges Tired Saudi Fields," *New York Times,* February 24, 2004. Kevin Phillips, *American Dynasty: Aristocracy, Fortune, and the Politics of Deceit in the House of Bush*, Viking, 2004.

18. See Kleveman, "Oil and the New 'Great Game.'"

19. See David Harvey, *The New Imperialism,* Oxford University Press, 2003.

20. Wallerstein in *Monthly Review* 55, no. 3, and in "Soft Multi-lateralism," *Nation,* February 2, 2004. See also Michael Klare, "The New Geopolitics," *Monthly Review* 55, no. 3 (July–August 2003).

21. See Peter Gowan, "U.S. Hegemony Today," *Monthly Review* 55, no. 3 (July–August 2003).

22. David Harvey, *The New Imperialism,* Oxford University Press, 2003 (especially chapter 2).

23. Chalmers Johnson, *The Sorrows of Empire: Militarism, Secrecy, and the End of the Republic,* Henry Holt and Co., 2004.

24. Chalmers Johnson, "America's Empire of Bases," http://www.americanempireproject.com.

25. See for example Ian Williams, "The Real National Security Threat: The Bush Economy," *Alternet,* January 13, 2004, http://alternet.org/story.html?StoryID=17547.

26. See Perry Anderson, "Force and Consent," Editorial, *New Left Review* 17 (September–October 2002) p. 6. See also Andrew J. Bacevich, *American Empire: The Realities and Consequences of U.S. Diplomacy,* Harvard University Press, 2004, for the argument that foreign policy from the first Bush administration through Clinton to the second Bush

administration has been dominated by the same key assumptions, a vision of growth and expansion, and the conviction that American values and interests should enjoy pride of place in the global order.

27. See Joshua Micah Marshall, "A Critic at Large: Power Rangers," *New Yorker,* February 2, 2004. See also Robin Blackburn, "Road to Armageddon," *Counterpunch,* October 3, 2001.

28. See Timothy Garton Ash, "The Peril of Too Much Power," *New York Times,* April 9, 2002.

29. See Stanley Hoffman, "France, the United States, and Iraq," *Nation,* February 16, 2004.

30. See Ivo H. Daalder and James M. Lindsay, *America Unbound: The Bush Revolution in Foreign Policy,* Brookings Institution Press, 2003.

31. The formulation is from Arundhati Roy, "The New American Century," *Nation,* February 9, 2004.

32. Eric Hobsbawm, "After the Winning of the War," *Le Monde Diplomatique*, June 2003.

33. See Serge Schmemann, "The Coalition of the Unbelieving," *New York Times Book Review*, January 25, 2004.

34. *New York Times*, February 5, 2004. The *Times* also reported a bipartisan study led by Edward P. Djerejian, a former ambassador to Israel and Syria, that concluded American international prestige had dwindled.

35. See James Traub, "It's Not that the Democrats Don't Have Sensible, Sophisticated Plans to Deal with Iraq . . ." *New York Times Magazine*, January 4, 2004.

36. See Robert Kagan, *Of Paradise and Power,*" Afterword, Vintage Books, 2004.

37. See Jeffrey Record, "Bounding the Global War on Terror-

ism," Strategic Studies Institute, U.S. Air Force College, posted on washingtonpost.com, January 12, 2004.

38. See Brian Urquhart, "Hidden Truths," *New York Review,* March 25, 2004.

39. See Jonathan Schell, "The Empire Backfires," *Nation,* March 12, 2004.

40. David Harvey, *The New Imperialism,* Oxford University Press, 2003, p. 17.

CHAPTER 2

1. Chalmers Johnson cites journalists Diana Johnstone and Ben Cramer: "If the danger [of a Soviet-American war in Europe] never really existed, then it can be argued that a primary mission of U.S. forces in Europe in reality has been to *maintain* the Soviet threat . . . and thus their double military hegemony over the European continent." *The Sorrows of Empire: Militarism, Secrecy, and the End of the Republic,* Henry Holt and Co., 2004, 33.

2. Johnson, ibid, 56.

3. See for example Juan Forero, "Private U.S. Operatives on Risky Missions in Columbia," *New York Times,* February 14, 2004.

4. See James Dao, "Private Guards Take Big Risks for Right Price," *New York Times,* April 2, 2004. See also Thom Shanker and Eric Schmitt, "Delivery Delays Hurt U.S. Effort to Equip Iraqis," *New York Times,* March 22, 2004; Eric Schmitt and Thom Shanker, "Big Pay Luring Military's Elite to Private Jobs," *New York Times,* March 30, 2004; and Bill Berkowitz, "Mercenaries 'R' Us," Alternet.org, March 24, 2004.

5. See Chalmers Johnson, "America's Empire of Bases," http://

americanempireproject.com. The Defense Department reports 702 bases but Johnson thinks an honest count would yield 1,000.

6. Ibid.

7. See Stansfield Turner, "Five Steps to Better Spying," *New York Times,* Op Ed, February 9, 2004; see also "Military Industrial: How Weapons Makers Are Shaping U.S. Foreign and Military Policies," June 20, 2002, http://www.foreign-policy-infocus.org/papers/micr/companies_body.html.

8. Ibid, 64.

9. See Military Industrial Complex Revisited, November 2001, http://www.foreignpolicyinfocus.org/papers/micr/notes_body .html/.

10. The new space mission announced by President Bush cost only $1 billion in new money over the next five years, presuming that $11 billion would come from other NASA programs. But the cost of establishing a base on the moon by 2020, which is what Bush proposed, is estimated to cost $150 billion or more. See Edmund Andrews, "Investing in the Future, and Mortgaging It," *New York Times,* January 18, 2004. American ambitions are suggested by the fact that in October 2002 the United States, along with Israel, voted against a UN resolution strengthening the 1967 Outer Space Treaty to ban use of space for military purposes, including offensive weapons. The United States and Israel also voted against a UN resolution calling for reaffirmation of a 1925 Geneva convention banning biological weapons. See Noam Chomsky and Michael Albert, "Interview," *Znet,* April 13, 2003, http://www.zmag.org/content/showarticle.cfm?Section1D+41&Item1D+3450.

11. Henry L. Stimson, *Diary,* August 26, 1940, Stimson Papers. Quoted in John F. Manley, "Who Can We Shoot? A Critique

of the Unexceptional American Welfare State." Unpublished paper.

12. The mergers were encouraged by Clinton administration Department of Defense officials who anticipated cutbacks from the Reagan military buildup of the 1980s. See Norman R. Augustine, "Reshaping an Industry: Lockheed Martin's Survival Story," *Harvard Business Review,* May–June 1997.

13. "Military Industrial Complex Revisited, June 20, 2002, http://www.foreignpolicy-infocus.org/papers/micr/notes_body .html.

14. Cited in Chalmers Johnson, *The Sorrows of Empire: Militarism, Secrecy, and the End of the Republic,* Henry Holt and Co., 2004, 39.

15. Naomi Klein, "Privatization in Disguise," *Nation,* April 28, 2003.

16. See Joel Brinkley and Eric Schmitt, "Halliburton Will Repay U.S. Excess Charges for Troops Meals," *New York Times,* February 3, 2004.

17. Jeff Gerth and Don Van Natta Jr., "Halliburton Contracts in Iraq: The Struggle to Manage Costs," *New York Times,* December 29, 2003. See also Jane Mayer, "Contract Sport: What Did the Vice-President Do for Halliburton?" *New Yorker,* February 16–23, 2004.

18. See Jane Mayer, "Contract Sport: What Did the Vice-President Do for Halliburton?" *New Yorker,* February 16–23, 2004.

19. See Bob Herbert, "The Halliburton Shuffle," *New York Times,* January 30, 2004.

20. See *Wall Street Journal,* January 7, 2004.

21. Center for Public Integrity, "Windfalls of War: U.S. Contractors in Iraq and Afghanistan," 2003, www.public integrity.org/wow/.

22. Richard A. Oppel Jr. "A Big Texas Contractor Prospered," *New York Times,* March 30, 2003.

23. Jane Mayer, "Contract Sport: What Did the Vice-President Do for Halliburton?" New Yorker, February 16–23, 2004.

24. See Arundhati Roy, "The New American Century," *The Nation,* February 9, 2004.

25. Kevin Phillips, *American Dynasty: Aristocracy, Fortune, and the Politics of Deceit in the House of Bush,* Viking, 2004.

26. "Kevin Phillips, Author of 'American Dynasty: Aristocracy, Fortune and the Politics of Deceit in the House of Bush.'" A Buzzflash Interview, January 7, 2004, BuzzFlash.com.

27. Prepared testimony delivered on February 12, 2003.

28. Leslie Wayne, "Pentagon Says It Plans to Kill Copter Program," *New York Times,* February 24, 2004.

29. General Accounting Office Testimony Before the Subcommittee on Readiness and Management Support, Committee on Armed Services, U.S. Senate, *DOD Financial Management: Integrated Approach, Accountability, Transparency, and Incentives Are Keys to Effective Reform,* March 6, 2002, GAO-02-497T.

30. Wesley Clark, "Iraq: What Went Wrong," *New York Review,* September 25, 2003. For a catalogue of high tech misspending in an era when no major power threatens the United States, see "Misspending Military Dollars," *New York Times,* Editorial, February 5, 2004.

31. See Jane Mayer, "Contract Sport," *New Yorker,* February 16–23, 2004, p. 90.

32. Johnson, *The Sorrows of Empire*, 60.

33. See Thomas E. Ricks, "For Zinni, a War that Ignores Facts," *Washington Post National Weekly Edition*, January 12–18, 2004.

34. Richard W. Stevenson, "Bush Sought to Oust Hussein from Start, Ex-Official Says," *New York Times,* January 12, 2004.

35. Richard A. Clarke, *Against All Enemies,* The Free Press, 2004.

36. See Seymour Hersh, "The Stovepipe," *New Yorker,* October 27, 2003; James Fallows, Seymour Hersh, *Atlantic Monthly,* January–February 2004.

37. The appellation is used by Patrick Buchanan in "Whose War? A Neo Conservative Clique Seeks to Ensnare Our Country in a Series of Wars that Are Not in America's Interest," *American Conservative,* March 24, 2003.

38. For an exhaustive examination of the role of these think tanks, see Dolores E. Janiewski, "Remaking the World: The New Right's Global Visions," unpublished manuscript, January 2004. See also David Brock, *Blinded by the Right: The Conscience of an Ex-Conservative,* Crown Publishers, 2002.

39. Daalder and Lindsay draw a distinction between the more visionary neo-cons who want to remake the world in America's image, and Cheney and Rumsfeld, who they see as hardboiled nationalists. But the two groups are allies in their advocacy of unilateral war. See Ivo H. Daalder and James M. Lindsay, *America Unbound: The Bush Revolution in Foreign Policy,* Brookings Institution Press, 2003.

40. *Washington Times* editor at large Arnoud de Borchgrave writes "Washington's 'Likudnmiks'" have been in charge of U.S. policy in the Middle East since Bush was sworn into office. See Buchanan, "Whose War?" *American Conservative,* March 24, 2003.

41. Cited in David Brock, *Blinded by the Right,* Crown Publishers, 2002, p. 50.

42. Ibid, 61.

43. Patrick Buchanan, "Whose War?" *American Conservative,* March 24, 2003.

44. See Buchanan, ibid. See also Janiewski, 134, and Max Boot, "Neo-cons," *Foreign Policy,* January–February 2004.

45. Also cited in Buchanan, "Whose War?" *American Conservative,* March 24, 2003.

46. Chalmers Johnson, "America's Empire of Bases," http://www.americanempireproject.com.

47. See Buchanan, "Whose War?" *American Conservative,* March 24, 2003.

48. Robert Jay Lifton, "American Apocalypse," *Nation,* December 22, 2003.

49. Irving Kristol, "The Neo-conservative Persuasion," *Weekly Standard,* August 25, 2003.

50. David Frum and Richard Perle, *An End to Evil: How to Win the War on Terror,* Random House, 2004.

51. See Robert Borosage, "Bush's Budget Lies," *Nation,* February 23, 2004.

52. See Richard Kogan, "The Omnibus Appropriations Bill: Are Appropriations for Domestic Programs Exploding?" Center on Budget and Policy Priorities, December 31, 2003. Kogan estimates the costs of the war alone at $120 billion in 2004. See "Sacrifice Is Relative," Center on Budget and Policy Priorities, September 11, 2003.

53. Ron Suskind, *The Price of Loyalty,* based on interviews and materials supplied by former Secretary of the Treasury Paul O'Neill, depicts administration decision-making as preoccupied with satisfying "the base."

54. See David D. Kirkpatrick, "A Concerned Bloc of Republicans Wonders Whether Bush Is Conservative Enough," *New York Times,* January 25, 2004.

55. See Elizabeth Drew, "The Enforcer," *New York Review,* 50, no. 7 (May 1, 2003). For a glimpse at Rove's astonishing record of dirty tricks in electoral campaigns see Anne S. Lewis, "Rove-ing Lunatic," *Austin Chronicle,* March 17, 2004.

56. See Grover Nordquist, "The Second Term Diet," *American Spectator,* March 2004.

57. See Michael Scherer, "The Soul of the New Machine," *Mother Jones,* January–February 2004, p. 46.

58. James Fallows captures this particular potential schism in a quote from Lawrence Sumners, Secretary of the Treasury in the Clinton administration: "September eleventh brings to the fore issues that no one is in favor of privatizing. National defense, protection against terrorism, maintaining public health, putting out fires: inevitably these will lead to greater appreciation of the need for a strong capable government. . . ." See "Councils of War," *Atlantic Monthly,* January 2002.

59. Rachel L. Swarns, "Outcry on Right Over Bush Plan on Immigration," *New York Times,* February 21, 2004.

60. General Wesley K. Clark, *Winning Modern Wars: Iraq, Terrorism, and the American Empire,* Public Affairs, 2003.

61. Meanwhile, Democrats more reliant on the "soft money" now restricted by campaign finance law have turned to new organizations called "527s," named for a section of the tax code, particularly for voter registration and turnout efforts. This practice, in turn, is under challenge at the Federal Elections Commission by the Republicans in another episode of an effort to "defund the left" that dates from the Reagan administration. See Harold Meyerson, "Numbers Game," *American Prospect,* March 2004.

62. Majorities in both houses of Congress are important, since they determine the size of staffs, offices, and committee assignments.

63. See Chalmers Johnson, *The Sorrows of Empire,* Holt and Co., 2004.

64. See Nicholas Lemann, "The Next World Order," *New Yorker,* April 1, 2002.

65. Perry Anderson, "Force and Consent," *New Left Review* 17 (September–October 2002) pp. 11–12.

66. "George W. Bush and the Real State of the Union," *London Guardian,* January 21, 2004.

67. Tom Purdum, "Leaders Face Challenges Far Different from Those of Last Conflict," *New York Times,* September 15, 2001.

68. Robert Jay Lifton, "American Apocalypse," *Nation*, December 22, 2003, p. 12.

69. See Michael Valpy, "Code Name Has Whiff of Brimstone," *Globe and Mail,* September 20, 2001.

70. Gary Wills, "With God on His Side," *New York Times Magazine,* March 20, 2003, p. 29.

71. Elizabeth Drew, "The Enforcer," *New Yorker*, 50, no. 7 (May 1, 2003).

72. Elizabeth Drew reports, drawing on data provided by pollster John Zogby, "that while there was much talk of a Republican sweep of both houses of Congress in 2002, several of the Senate races were quite close, and many of the voters made up their minds on election morning. See Elizabeth Drew, "Hung Up in Washington," *New York Review,* February 12, 2004, p. 17. See also Drew, "The Enforcer," ibid.

73. Chris Cillizza and Lauren W. Whittington, "House and Senate Races Lack Passion of White House Election: GOP Favored," *Roll Call,* January 20, 2004.

74. See Harold Meyerson, "Numbers Game," *American Prospect,* March 2004. From the days of the Reagan administration, the Republicans have periodically made attempts to "defund

the left" by challenging the tax status of NGOs that take political positions.

75. See David E. Rosenbaum, "Congressional Redistricting Battle Could Lead to New Rules," *New York Times,* February 23, 2004, and "Elections with No Meaning," *New York Times,* Editorial, February 21, 2003.

76. Cited in Paul Krugman, *The Great Unraveling: Losing Our Way in the New Century,* Norton, 2003, p. 17.

77. Quoted in Elisabeth Bumiller; "The President Sets Out Danger as a Campaign Theme," *New York Times,* "Week in Review," January 24, 2004.

78. Richard W. Stevenson, "Campaign Begins as Bush Attacks Kerry in Speech," *New York Times,* February 24, 2004.

79. Tony Walker, "Backroom Operator Wields Most Power," *Australian Financial Review,* November 28, 2003.

80. *Newsweek* Poll (August–September 2004), cited in *Tomeditor* dispatch, http://1w12fd.law12.hotmail.msn.com/cgibin/get-msg?msg=MSG1075081810.4&mfs=&_ .

CHAPTER 3

1. Quoted in Paul Krugman, "Looting the Future," *New York Times,* December 5, 2003.

2. See Naomi Klein, "Bring Halliburton Home," *Nation,* November 24, 2003; and Naomi Klein, "Risky Business," *Nation,* January 5, 2004.

3. See David Bacon, "The U.S. Arrests Iraq's Union Leaders," December 10, 2003 dbacon@igc.org, and David Bacon, "The Occupation's War on Iraqi Workers," *Portside,* November 26, 2003, http://www.yahoogroups.com/group/portside.

4. See Klein, "Risky Business," *Nation,* January 5, 2004.

5. See Frances Fox Piven and Richard A. Cloward, *The New Class War: Reagan's Attack on the Welfare State and Its Consequences,* Pantheon Books, 1982, chapter 1.

6. See Jayati Ghosh, "Understanding the Effects of U.S. Neoliberalism," *Frontline: India's National Magazine* 21, no. 5 (February 28–March 12, 2004).

7. On the fundamentals of "Clintonomics," see Robert Pollin, *Contours of Descent: U.S. Economic Fractures and the Landscape of Global Austerity, Verso Books,* London, 2003.

8. See "Economic Stimulus," Stimulus Coalition, www.ourfuture.org.

9. Joel Friedman, "The Decline of Corporate Income Tax Revenues," Center on Budget and Policy Priorities, October 24, 2003.

10. See Carl Hulse and David Firestone, "On the Hill: Budget Business as Usual," *New York Times,* March 23, 2003.

11. See James A. Parrott, "The Coming Fiscal Train Wreck," *New Labor Forum* 12, no. 3 (Fall 2003); Harold Meyerson, "Good for Investors: Bad for the Rest," *Washington Post,* January 14, 2004; Paul Krugman, *The Great Unraveling: Losing Our Way in the New Century,* Norton, 2003.

12. Richard S. Dunham and Mike McNamee, with Howard Gleckman and Paul Magnusson, "Jobs: Desperately Seeking Answers," *Business Week,* March 8, 2004.

13. See Richard A. Oppel Jr., "Budget Office Predicts Deficit Over 10 Years: $2.75 Trillion," *New York Times,* February 28, 2004.

14. See James A. Parrott, The Coming Fiscal Train Wreck," New Labor Forum 12, no. 3 (Fall 2003). See also Liz McNichol, "The State Fiscal Crisis: Extent, Causes, and Responses," Center on Budget and Policy Priorities, April 24, 2003; and see Mike Hall, "Paying the Price for Bush Policies: State and

Local Workers Fight Privatization," America@Work, December 2003.

15. Paul Krugman, *The Great Unraveling: Losing Our Way in the New Century;* Norton, 2003, 187.

16. Ibid. Krugman, p. 9.

17. Cited in David R. Francis, "U.S. Moves—quietly—Toward a Flat Tax," *Christian Science Monitor*, December 1, 2003. As Francis points out, at the top the tax system has already become regressive because the super-rich pay proportionately less than the merely rich.

18. David Callahan, "Take Back Values," *Nation,* February 9, 2004.

19. See General Accounting Office, "Internal Revenue Service: Challenges Remain in Combatting Abusive Tax Shelters," Testimony Before the Committee on Finance, U.S. Senate, October 21, 2003. See also Jonathan Weisman, "GAO Finds Increase in Tax Evasion," *Washington Post,* December 19, 2003.

20. See Edmund L. Andrews, "Bush Budget Cuts or Cancels School Programs, Drug Centers and Air Traffic Changes," *New York Times,* February 4, 2004.

21. See Joel Friedman, "The Decline of Corporate Income Tax Revenues," Center on Budget and Policy Priorities, October 24, 2003.

22. Isaac Shapiro, "Federal Income Taxes, as a Share of GDP, Drop to Lowest Level Since 1942, According to Budget Data," Center on Budget and Policy Priorities, October 21, 2003.

23. William D. Nordhaus, "The Story of a Bubble," *New York Review of Books,* January 15, 2004.

24. See John S. Irons, "Half of 2004 Deficit Deterioration Due to Revenue-Reduction Legislation," OMB Watch, September 3, 2003, www.ombwatch.org.

25. Paul Krugman, "Who Lost the U.S. Budget?" *New York Times,* March 21, 2003.

26. See Floyd Norris, "Help Grandparents of Rich Kids Now, Deal with Real Problems Later," *Washington Post National Weekly*, February 6, 2004.

27. Martin Muhleisen and Christopher Towe, editors, "U.S. Fiscal Policies and Priorities for Long-Run Sustainability," Occasional Paper 227, International Monetary Fund, January 7, 2004.

28. Paul Krugman, "Red Ink Realities," *New York Times,* January 27, 2004.

29. "Mr. Greenspan's Warning," *New York Times,* Editorial, February 27, 2004.

30. See Public Agenda Alert, February 26, 2004, http://www.publicagenda.org.

31. Both of these quotes come from Robert Greenstein and Isaac Shapiro, "Taking Down the Toll Booth to the Middle Class?" Center on Budget and Policy Priorities, February 6, 2001.

32. For a discussion and data, see Larry M. Bartels, "Homer Gets a Tax Cut: Inequality and Public Policy in the American Mind," prepared for presentation at the Annual Meeting of the American Political Science Association, Philadelphia, August 2003.

33. "Income Watch: The Rich are Getting Richer and Getting Bigger Tax Breaks," OMB Watch, January 7, 2004, http://www.ombwatch.org/article/view/1615/1/2/.

34. See Richard A. Oppel, Budget Office Predicts Deficit Over 10 Years: $2.75 Trillion," *New York Times*, February 28, 2004. The administration's budget also omits a number of other domestic budget items. See Richard Kogan and Rob-

ert Greenstein, "Sanitizing the Grim News: The Administration's Efforts to Make Harmful Deficits Appear Benign," Center on Budget and Policy Priorities, July 18, 2003.

35. See "Disturbing Pattern Emerging on Government Budget Analyses," OMB Watch, January 7, 2004, http://www.ombwatch.org/article/view/1720/1/2/. The Center on Budget and Policy Priorities makes a similar critique of government estimates of deficits and expenditures. See Richard Kogan, "Will the President's 2005 Budget Really Cut the Deficit in Half?" January 16, 2004.

36. Holly Sklar, "Upper-Class Tax Cuts: Working-Class Soldiers," Alternet, April 11, 2003, http://www.alternet.org/story.html?StoryID=15616.

37. See Elisabeth Bumiller, "Bush Takes Tax Cut Battle on the Road," *New York Times,* April 25, 2003.

38. Molly Ivins, "The Uncompassionate Conservative," *Mother Jones,* November–December 2003.

39. Joel Bleifuss, "The Sludge Hits the Fan," *In These Times,* March 18, 2004.

40. See Bob Williams and Kevin Bogardus, "The Politics of Energy: Oil and Gas," Special Report from The Center for Public Integrity, 2002.

41. See Kevin Bogardus, "The Politics of Energy: Nuclear Power," Special Report from The Center for Public Integrity, 2002; and see Bruce Barcoff, "Changing the Rules," *New York Times Magazine,* April 4, 2004.

42. See Christopher Drew and Richard A. Oppel Jr., "How Power Lobby Won Battle of Pollution Control at EPA," *New York Times,* March 6, 2004.

43. David G. Savage and Richard A. Serrano, "Scalia Was Cheney Hunt Trip Guest," *Los Angeles Times,* February 5, 2004.

44. "Beyond the Duck Blind," *New York Times,* March 15, 2004.

45. Neil Lewis, "Federal Judge Orders Release of Documents of White House Task Force on Energy," *New York Times,* April 2, 2004.

46. See Williams and Bogardus, "The Politics of Energy: Oil and Gas," Special Report from the Center for Public Integrity 2002; Bogardus, The Politics of Energy: Nuclear Power," Special Report from the Center for Public Integrity, 2002; Bob Allison, Kevin Bogardus, Alex Cohen, Bernadette Cullen, and Bill Dawson, "The Politics of Energy: Coal," The Center for Public Integrity, November 21, 2003; "No Pig Left Behind," *Nation,* Editorial, December 15, 2003.

47. Barcoff, "Changing the Rules," *New York Times Magazine,* April 4, 2004.

48. See Ron Suskind, *The Price of Loyalty: George W. Bush, the White House, and the Education of Paul O'Neill,* Simon and Schuster, 2004.

49. See "Warming Up," *New York Times,* Editorial, January 25, 2004.

50. Charles J. Hanley, "CO2 Hits Record Levels, Researchers Find," *Associated Press,* March 20, 2004.

51. Bogardus, "The Politics of Energy: Nuclear Power," Special Report from the Center for Public Integrity, 2002, p. 2.

52. See Eric Pianin, "Thanks for the Memos: Proposed Mercury Rules Resemble what the Utility Lawyers Wrote," *Washington Post National Weekly Edition.*

53. Jennifer Lee, "Most States Expect Pollution to Rise if Regulations Change," *New York Times,* February 6, 2004.

54. See Bruce Barcoff, "Changing the Rules, *New York Times Magazine,* April 4, 2004" and "Stirrings on Clean Air," Editorial, *New York Times,* March 27, 2004.

55. Chalmers Johnson, "America's Empire of Bases," 2004, http://www.americanempireproject.com/.

56. See Jennifer S. Lee, "Drop in Budget Slows Superfund Program," *New York Times,* March 9, 2004.

57. Mark Hertsgaard, "The Once-Green GOP," *Nation,* February 9, 2004.

58. "The War at Home," *New York Times,* Editorial, February 12, 2004.

59. Jennifer S. Lee, "U.S. Drops Forest Rule," *New York Times,* March 24, 2004.

60. "An Environmental Deficit," *New York Times,* Editorial, February 11, 2004.

61. See "No Pig Left Behind," *Nation,* Editorial, December 15, 2003.

62. "Buying Public Policy," *Lowdown,* 6, no. 1 (January 2004).

63. Robert Pear, "Senators Threaten to Delay Action on Medicare Nominee," *New York Times,* February 25, 2004.

64. Robert Pear, "Medicare Nominee Backs Drug Imports," *New York Times,* March 9, 2004.

65. Sheryl Gay Stolberg, "Senate Democrats Block Caps for Malpractice," *New York Times,* February 25, 2004. See also "The Gun Lobby's Bull's-Eye," *New York Times,* Editorial, February 25, 2004.

66. See Robert W. McChesney, "The Escalating War Against Corporate Media," *Monthly Review.* 55, no. 10 (March 2004) p. 12. See also by McChesney, *The Problem of the Media: U.S. Communication Politics in the Twenty-First Century,* Monthly Review Press, 2004.

67. See McChesney, "The Escalating War," *Monthly Review* 55, no. 10 (March 2004), p. 12. McChesney describes the emergence of something like a citizen's movement over the issue.

68. John Nichols, "When Rupert Murdoch Calls . . ." *Nation,* March 25, 2004.

69. See Michael R. Bloomberg, Richard M. Daley, James K. Hahn, and Scott L. King, "Lawyers, Guns and Mayors," *New York Times,* February 24, 2004.

70. Carl Hulse, "After Disputes Congress Passes Spending Plan," *New York Times,* January 23, 2004.

71. Sheryl Gay Stolbert, "Looking Back and Ahead After Senate's Votes on Guns," *New York Times,* March 4, 2004.

72. Paul Krugman, "Strictly Business," *New York Review,* November 20, 2003.

73. Donald G. McNeil, "U.S. Scientist Tells of Pressure to Lift Bans on Food Imports," *New York Times,* February 25, 2004.

74. Ibid.

75. "Take Their Advice," *New York Times*, Editorial, February 6, 2004.

76. Tomeditor, "The Big Cheese Stands Alone," February 29, 2004, Tomeditor@aol.com.

77. Sandra Blakeslee, "Plan for Sharp Rise in Mad Cow Testing Gets Mixed Reaction," *New York Times,* March 17, 2004.

78. "A Triumph for Big Sugar," *New York Times,* February 14, 2004.

79. Andrew C. Revkin, "U.S. Requests Exemptions to Ozone Pact for Chemical," *New York Times,* March 4, 2004.

80. Robert F. Kennedy Jr., "The Junk Science of George W. Bush," *Nation,* March 8, 2004. See also Eric Alterman and Mark Green, "The New Scopes Trials," *Nation,* March 8, 2004.

81. Geoffrey Lean, "Global Warming Spirals Upwards," *Independent,* March 28, 2004.

82. Sheryl Gay Stolberg, "When Spin Spins Out of Control," *New York Times,* March 21, 2004.

83. There were scientists lined up on both sides of this issue. See Charles Tilly, *Social Movements,* 1768–2004, Paradigm Publishers, 2004, pp. 10–11.

84. Jennifer Lee, "White House Minimized the Risks of Mercury in Proposed Rules, Scientists Say," *New York Times,* April 7, 2004.

85. Quoted in Eric Alterman and Mark Green, "The New Scopes Trials," *Nation,* March 8, 2004.

86. Ibid.

87. See James Glanz, "Scientists: Bush Administration Distorts Facts," *TODAY @ abs-cbnNEWS.com,* February 24, 2004.

88. "Uses and Abuses of Science," *New York Times*, Editorial, January 23, 2004. The White House has issued a rebuttal to these accusations. See Andrew C. Revkin, "Bush's Science Aide Rejects Claims of Distorted Facts," *New York Times,* April 3, 2004.

89. Andrew C. Revkin, "Bush's Science Aide Rejects Claims of Distorted Facts," *New York Times,* April 3, 2004.

90. Trish Nicholson, "Kiss Your Overtime Pay Goodbye," *AARP Bulletin,* February 2004; Working Families e-Activist Network, AFL-CIO January 8, 2004.

91. Shawn Zeller, "Unions Object to Pentagon Labor-Management Proposal," February 6, 2004, http://www.gov exec.com/dailyfed/010604sz1.htm. Actually the administration first proposed eliminating civil service and collective bargaining protections for Department of Defense workers in April 2003. This and many of the specific items that follow in the discussion of labor rights are taken from the AFL-CIO report, "The Bush Administration Record," prepared by the AFL-CIO Public Policy Department, February 2003. Extensive documentation is provided on the BushWatch section of the AFL-CIO website, www.aflcio.org.

92. See James Parks, "Bargaining in Tough Times," America@Work, January–February 2004; Jane Birnbaum, "No Wage to Low Wage," America@Work, January–February 2004.

93. See David Bacon, "A Heroic Defense and a Cruel System," Alternet, March 10, 2004, http://groups.yahoo.com/group /portside/; Steven Greenhouse, "Labor Is Feeling Embattled as Union Leaders Convene," New York Times, March 9, 2004. Under the new contract signed by the supermarket workers, new workers would have a lower wage and only bare bones health coverage.

94. See "The Buying of the President 2004: Who Bankrolls Bush and His Democratic Rivals?" The Center for Public Integrity, February 12, 2004, http://www.bop2004/report.aspx?aid= 132.

95. Jesse Eisinger, "Year of the (Shrugged Off) Scandal," Wall Street Journal, January 2, 2004.

CHAPTER 4

1. David Brooks, "More than Money," New York Times, March 2, 2004.

2. The quote is from A Charge to Keep: My Journey to the White House, p. 229–30, cited by www.issues2000.org.

3. Richard Kogan, "Left Behind in Good Times and Bad: Administration's 2003 Budget Proposes Reductions in Programs for Low- and Moderate-Income Families Amidst an Economic Slump," Center on Budget and Policy Priorities, Revised January 28, 2003. The quote is from p. 2.

4. See Richard Kogan and David Kamin, "President's Budget Contains Larger Cuts in Domestic Discretionary Programs:

OMB Documents Not Made Widely Available Show Domestic Discretionary Programs to Be Cut $50 Billion a Year by 2009," Center on Budget and Policy Priorities, February 11, 2004.

5. States can allocate unspent TANF money to other allowed poverty-related programs, but there is in fact evidence the states have simply diverted TANF dollars by replacing state funds for welfare with federal TANF funds. See Pietro S. Nivola, Jennifer L. Noyes, and Isabel V. Sawhill, "Waive of the Future? Federalism and the Next Phase of Welfare Reform," *Brookings Institution Policy Brief*, no. 29 (March 2004).

6. Richard Kogan and Robert Greenstein, "Analysis of the President's Budget," Center on Budget and Policy Priorities, Revised February 11, 2004.

7. Ibid, p. 29.

8. Center on Budget and Policy Priorities Issue Alert, March 5, 2004.

9. "760,000 Jobless Denied Aid—and Counting," Center on Budget and Policy Priorities, February 25, 2004.

10. See David Hilfiker, "The Stealth Attack on the Poor," *New Labor Forum* 12, no. 3 (Fall 2003).

11. See National Alliance to End Homelessness Online Newsletter, March 5, 2004, http://www.endhomelessness.org/pub/onlinenews/2004/news03-05-04.pdf.

12. See Jack Newfield, "Bush to City: Drop Dead," *Nation,* April 19, 2004.

13. See National Low-Income Housing Coalition, "Call to Action," February 4, 2004; Media Advisory, February 12, 2004; and "Memo to Members," weekly newsletter of the National Low-Income Housing Coalition, 9, no. 9 (March 5, 2004).

14. See Robert Pear, "Sluggish Start for Offer of Tax Credit for Insurance," *New York Times,* January 25, 2004.

15. Robert Pear, "Inquiry Finds Sharp Increase in Health Insurance Schemes, *New York Times,* March 3, 2004.

16. See Jonathan Cohn, "How Medicaid Was Set Adrift," *New York Times,* March 6, 2004; David Hilfiker, "The Stealth Attack on the Poor," *New Labor Forum* 12, no. 3 (Fall 2003).

17. See Robert Pear, "U.S. Nears Clash with Governors on Medicaid Cost," *New York Times,* February 16, 2004; Robert Pear, "Bush to Revisit Changes in Medicaid Rules," *New York Times,* February 23, 2004.

18. See David Hilfiker, "The Stealth Attack on the Poor," *New Labor Forum* 12, no. 3 (Fall 2003).

19. Last year, some 400,000 people were caught crossing the border illegally in Arizona. Charges were brought against about 3,000 of them. So entrenched is the border crossing pattern and its hazards that smugglers are now offering three trips across the border for a flat rate in case people are caught on the first two trips. See Eric Lichtblau, "As Border Woes Strain Arizona, U.S. and Mexico Talk," *New York Times,* March 29, 2004.

20. Mike Davis, "Bush and the Great Wall," January 19, 2004, Tomeditor@aol.com.

21. See Doris Meissner, "U.S. Temporary Worker Programs: Lessons Learned," Migration Information Source, Migration Policy Institute, March 1, 2004.

22. See Elisabeth Bumiller, "Bush Would Give Illegal Workers Broad New Rights," *New York Times,* January 7, 2004; "Temporary Immigration," *New York Times,* Editorial, January 12, 2004; Robert Kuttner, "Bush's Cynical Immigration Gambit," *BusinessWeek,* February 9, 2004. See also Maia Jachi-

mowicz, "Bush Proposes New Temporary Worker Program," Migration Information Source, Migration Policy Institute, February 1, 2004, and Elizabeth Grieco and Brian Ray, "Mexican Immigrants in the U.S. Labor Force," Migration Information Source, Migration Policy Institute, March 1, 2004.

23. Quoted in Steven Greenhouse, "Business Cheers Bush's Plan to Hire Immigrants More Easily, but Labor Is Wary," *New York Times,* January 8, 2004.

24. AFL-CIO, "Bush Immigration Proposal 'Creates a Permanent Underclass,'" January 11, 2004, http://www.aflcio. org/issuespolitics/immigration/ns01072004.cfm?RenderFor Print=1.

25. Ibid.

26. Elisabeth Bumiller, "Border Politics as Bush Woos 2 Key Groups with Proposal," *New York Times,* January 8, 2004.

27. Louis Uchitelle, "States Pay for Jobs, but It Doesn't Always Pay Off," *New York Times,* November 10, 2003.

28. Cited in Holly Sklar, "Upper-Class Tax Cuts: Working-Class Soldiers," *Alternet,* April 11, 2003, http://www.alternet. org/story.html?ID=15616.

29. See Iris J. Lav, "Federal Policies Contribute to the Severity of the State Fiscal Crisis," Center on Budget and Policy Priorities, December 3, 2003. See also Leighton Ku and Sashi Nimalendran, "Losing Out: States Are Cutting 1.2 to 1.6 Million Low-Income People from Medicaid, SCHIP, and Other State Health Insurance Programs," Center on Budget and Policy Priorities, December 22, 2003.

30. Federal Homeland Security grants to the states were actually directed to smaller states. This was much more likely to be a reflection of the interests of congressional Republicans than of estimates of where terrorists were likely to attack. New

York received $1.38 per capita, while Wyoming got $9.78. See Dale Russakoff and Rene Sanchez, "Begging, Borrowing for Security," *Washington Post,* April 1, 2004.

31. See Iris J. Lav, "Federal Policies Contribute to the Severity of the State Fiscal Crisis," Center on Budget and Policy Priorities, December 3, 2003. A number of the program cuts reported below are detailed in this article. See also OMB Watch, "Children Bear Brunt of Federal Tax Cuts," http://www.ombwatch.org/article/view/1703/1/2/.

32. Harold Meyerson, "No New Taxes," *LA Weekly,* January 15, 2004.

33. John M. Broder, "Schwarzenegger Budget Denies Some Health Care," *New York Times,* January 18, 2004.

34. See Bob Herbert, "The Other America," *New York Times,* January 23, 2004.

35. See Ku and Nimalendran, "Losing Out: States Are Cutting 1.2 to 1.6 million Low-Income People From Medicaid, SCHIP, and Other State Health Insurance Programs," Center on Budget and Policy Priorities, December 22, 2003, p. 15.

36. Ibid, p. 11.

37. See Pietro S. Nivola, Jennifer L. Noyes, and Isabel V. Sawhill, "Waive of the Future?" Federalism and the Next Phase of Welfare Reform," Brookings Institution Policy Brief, no. 29 (March 2004).

38. Edmund L. Andrews, "Bush Budget Cuts or Cancels School Programs, Drug Centers, and Air Traffic Changes," *New York Times,* February 4, 2004.

39. See Robert Borosage, "Bush's Budget Lies," *Nation,* February 23, 2004.

40. See "States in 3rd Year of Unprecedented Continuing Fiscal

Crisis; AFT Report: Cuts in Education, Healthcare Will Have Long-Term Effect," U.S. Newswire, February 12, 2004.

41. See OMB Watch, "State Supported Colleges and Universities See Massive Tuition Increase," http://www.ombwatch.org/article/view/1658/1/2/.

42. See "The Long-Term Budget Outlook," Congress of the United States, Congressional Budget Office, December 2003.

43. See Harold Meyerson, "Powerlines," *LA Weekly,* November 28–December 4, 2003.

44. See Theda Skocpol, "A Bad Senior Moment," *American Prospect,* January 2004.

45. Elizabeth Drew, "Hung Up in Washington," *New York Review,* February 12, 2004.

46. See "The Long-Term Budget Outlook," Congress of the United States, Congressional Budget Office, December 2003, and "Budget Issues: Long-Term Fiscal Challenges," Statement of David M. Walker, Controller General of the United States, General Accounting Office, February 27, 2004.

47. See "Who Bankrolls Bush," Center for Public Integrity, February 12, 2004.

48. Ibid.

49. See Paul Krugman, "Social Security Scares," *New York Times,* March 5, 2004; Marc Weisbrot, "Social Security Doing Just Fine," *Providence Journal,* January 23, 2004.

50. See "State of the Union," *New York Times,* Editorial, January 21, 2004.

51. "Budgetary Shock and Awe," *New York Times,* Editorial, March 25, 2003.

CHAPTER 5

1. The count was done by Cokie Roberts of ABC. See "The President Enters Credibility Gap," Tomeditor@aol.com, February 10, 2004.

2. Jim Rutenberg, "Bush Ad Campaign Ready to Kick Off an Expensive Effort," *New York Times,* March 4, 2004.

3. Lee Walczak, with Richard S. Dunham and Paula Dwyer in Washington, "Super Tuesday? That Was Kid Stuff," *Business-Week,* March 15, 2004, p. 38.

4. Richard W. Stevenson and Adam Nagourney, "Bush's Campaign Emphasizes Role of Leader in War," *New York Times,* March 17, 2004.

5. Elisabeth Bumiller, "Bush Says Thank You in Visit to the Troops," *New York Times,* March 19, 2004.

6. Nick Madigan and Katharine Q. Seelye, "Cheney Attacks Kerry's Record on the Military," *New York Times,* March 18, 2004.

7. Jim Rutenberg and David E. Sanger, "Bush Campaign Goes on Attack in New Anti-Kerry Ads," *New York Times,* March 12, 2004. See also Richard W. Stevenson and Adam Nagourney, "Bush's Campaign Emphasizes Role of Leader in War," *New York Times,* March 17, 2004.

8. Quoted in *Lowdown,* 5, no. 5 (May 2003).

9. Quoted in "Distorting the Intelligence," *New York Times,* Editorial, February 17, 2004. See also *Washington Post,* January 28, 2004. A similar scandal has overtaken the Blair administration in Great Britain. See John Cassidy, "The David Kelly Affair," *New Yorker,* December 8, 2003.

10. Official White House Transcript, March 17, 2003.

11. Jonathan Schell, "The Empire Backfires," *Nation,* March 12, 2004.

12. Thomas L. Friedman, "Axis of Appeasement," *New York Times,* March 18, 2004.

13. Thom Shanker and Eric Schmitt, "GI Toll Is Rising as Insurgents Try Wilier Bombs and Tactics," *New York Times,* March 15, 2004. See also "Iraqi Suicide Bombing Wounds 7 as Number of Daily Attacks Rises," *New York Times,* March 31, 2004.

14. "Wave of Attacks Shows No Sign of Letup," was the subtitle in a *New York Times* report of eleven new Iraqi police deaths in late March 2004. See Jeffrey Gettleman, "11 Iraqi Police Officers Are Killed by Gunmen," *New York Times,* March 24, 2004.

15. See Philip Connors, "Inside Baghdad's House of Fear," *Newsday,* February 22, 2004; Tom Hundley, "Families Wait in Vain for Promised Release: Frustration Grows Outside Prison," *Chicago Tribune,* January 9, 2004; Jeffrey Fleishman, "Iraqis Are Bitter Over U.S. Held Prisoners," *Los Angeles Times,* January 8, 2004; Christian Parenti, "Al Jazeera Goes to Jail: In Iraq's Media War, U.S. Troops Are Imprisoning and Abusing Arab Journalists," *Nation,* March 29, 2004.

16. Robert Fisk, "One Year On—War Without End," *London Independent,* March 14, 2004.

17. "One Year After," *New York Times,* Editorial, March 19, 2004.

18. This was a downward revision of the initial estimate of casualties. See John F. Burns, "Car Bomb at Baghdad Hotel Leaves at Least 27 Dead," *New York Times,* March 18, 2004, and also by Burns, "Hotel Attacks Linked to War Anniversary," *New York Times,* March 19, 2004.

19. Dexter Filkins, "Up to 16 Die in Gun Battles in Sunni Areas of Iraq," *New York Times,* March 27, 2004.

20. John F. Burns, "The Long Shadow of a Mob," *New York Times,* April 4, 2004.

21. Sami Ramadani, "Resistance to the Occupation Will Grow," *Guardian,* December 15, 2003. See also "CIA Warns of Possible Civil War in Iraq," *Hindustan Times,* January 24, 2004.

22. Jeffrey Gettleman, "G.I.s Padlock Baghdad Paper Accused of Lies," *New York Times,* March 29, 2004.

23. Jeffrey Gettleman, "An Incendiary Cleric Braces His Militia for an Invasion," *New York Times,* April 6, 2004.

24. "Killing Iraq with Kindness," *New York Times,* March 17, 2004.

25. Jeffrey Gettleman, "Chaos and War Leave Iraq's Hospitals in Ruins," *New York Times,* February 14, 2004; "One Year After," *New York Times,* Editorial, March 19, 2004.

26. See John F. Burns, "The Road Ahead May Be Even Rougher," *New York Times,* March 7, 2004. Estimates of the numbers dead as a result of these assaults vary from 140 to 200.

27. Certainly the American armed forces will not withdraw from the new bases that are now being constructed, which some analysts see as a main reason for the war. A "Status of Forces Agreement" between the Iraq Governing Council and the United States contemplates 100,000 or more American troops remaining in Iraq. See Phyllis Bennis, "The Iraqi Constitution and Events in Spain," Talking Points 15, United for Peace and Justice, March 16, 2004. A document released by the occupation authority in March 2004 read: "All trained elements of the Iraqi armed forces shall at all times be under the operational control of the commander of coalition forces for the purpose of conducting combined operations." See John F. Burns and Thom Shanker, "U.S. Officials Fashion Legal Basis to Keep Force in Iraq," *New York Times,* March

26, 2004. Just how many bases the United States is planning to establish in Iraq is disputed. Christine Spolar of the *Chicago Tribune* writes of "14 'enduring' bases set in Iraq," http://story.news.yahoo.com/news/tmpl = story&u = chitrib ts/20040323/ts_chicagotrib/14enduringbasessetiniraq&cic = 2027&ncid = 1473.

28. See the several reports by Dexter Filkins, "Iraq Council, with Reluctant Shiites, Signs Charter," *New York Times,* March 9, 2004; "Top Shiites Drop Their Resistance to Iraqi Charter," *New York Times,* March 8, 2004; "Iraqi Shiites, in a Blow to U.S., Fail to Sign Temporary Charter," *New York Times,* March 6, 2004.

29. John F. Burns, "U.S. Calls for Sunni and Kurdish Rights After Turnover," *New York Times,* March 25, 2004; and also by Burns, "Cleric May Warn Iraqis to Reject New Government, *New York Times,* March 28, 2004.

30. Phyllis Bennis, "The Iraqi Constitution and Events in Spain," Talking Points 15, United For Peace and Justice, March 16, 2004.

31. Dexter Filkins, "Some Iraqi Leaders Now Balk at Giving U.N. a Big Role," *New York Times,* March 15, 2004; John F. Burns, "Shiite Ayatollah Is Warning U.N. Against Endorsing Charter Sponsored by U.S." *New York Times,* March 23, 2004.

32. "New Attacks in Afghanistan Raise Concerns About Security," *New York Times,* March 29, 2004. "Terror in Tashkent," *New York Times,* Editorial, April 5, 2004.

33. David Rohde, "U.S. Announces New Offensive Against Taliban and Al Qaeda," *New York Times,* March 14, 2004.

34. See Amy Waldman, "Official Killed as Strife Grows in Afghanistan," *New York Times,* March 22, 2004, and "Kabul Sends Force to Quell Disorders After Killing," *New York*

Times, March 23, 2004; and Carlotta Gall, "Father of Slain Afghan Minister Demands Government Action," *New York Times,* March 24, 2004.

35. Ahmed Rashid, "The Mess in Afghanistan," *New York Review,* February 12, 2004.

36. James Benet, "Palestinians Swear Vengeance for Killing of Cleric by Israelis," *New York Times,* March 23, 2004; Neil MacFarquhar, "Wave of Anger Rolls Across Arab World," *New York Times,* March 23, 2004.

37. Seth Mydans, "3rd Day of Violence Claims 23 Lives in Uzbekistan," *New York Times,* March 31, 2004.

38. These developments are summarized in "Quotes for the First Anniversary of the Beginning of the Most Recent Iraqi War," March 19, 2004, Tomeditor@aol.com.

39. Schell, "The Empire Backfires," *Nation,* March 12, 2004.

40. "Whodunnit?" *Economist,* January 31, 2004.

41. Douglas Jehl and Eric Schmitt, "Rumsfeld and Tenet Defending Assessments of Iraqi Weapons," *New York Times,* February 5, 2004; "The Administration's Scramble," *New York Times,* Editorial, February 6, 2004.

42. Carnegie Endowment for International Peace, "WMD in Iraq: Evidence and Implications," January 2004.

43. Jim Lobe, *Asia Times,* February 3, 2004.

44. Jim Lobe, "The Day Cheney Was Rocked to the Core," *Asia Times online,* February 7, 2004. See also Chalmers Johnson, "Improve the CIA? Better to Abolish It," *San Francisco Chronicle,* February 22, 2004.

45. Douglas Jehl, "After Two Months, Bush's Panel on Prewar Iraq Starts to Stir," *New York Times,* April 2, 2004.

46. Scott Armstrong, "15 Questions," *New York Times,* April 4, 2004.

47. Paul Krugman makes this point. See "Weak on Terror," *New*

York Times, March 16, 2004. See also Steven Weisman, "Powell Wants Pakistani Help in Chasing Taliban Remnants," *New York Times,* March 16, 2004.

48. See Elisabeth Bumiller, "Want a Reliable President? Here's One You Can Set Your Clocks By," *New York Times,* March 15, 2004. See also the series of articles by Philip Shenon in the *New York Times:*"Bush in Reversal, Supports More Time for 9/11 Inquiry," February 5, 2005; "9/11 Panel Threatens to Issue Subpoena for Bush's Briefings," February 10, 2004; "9/11 Panel Rejects White House Limits on Interviews," March 3, 2004.

49. Philip Shenon, "Clinton Aides Plan to Tell Panel of Warning Bush Team on Qaeda," *New York Times,* March 20, 2004; David Sirota, Christy Harvey, and Judd Legum, "White House Tailspin," Progress Report, Independent Media Institute, March 23, 2004; Elisabeth Bumiller and Judith Miller, "Ex-Bush Aide Finding Fault Sets Off Debate," *New York Times,* March 23, 2004; Philip Shenon and Eric Schmitt, "Bush and Clinton Aides Grilled by Panel," *New York Times,* March 24, 2004.

50. Sheryl Gay Stolberg, "9/11 Widows Skillfully Applied the Power of a Question: Why?" *New York Times,* April 1, 2004.

51. Philip Shenon and Richard W. Stevenson, "Ex-Bush Aide Says Threat of Qaeda Was Not Priority," *New York Times,* March 25, 2004.

52. See Mathew Stannard, "Daniel Ellsberg Sees a New Trend—Telling All While the Issue Is Hot," *San Francisco Chronicle,* March 29, 2004. Ellsberg cited as examples Scott Ritter, Hans Blix, Paul O'Neill, Rand Beers, Joseph Wilson, John Brady Kiesling, Ray McGovern, Anthony Zinni, Karen Kwiatkowski, and in England, Robin Cook, Katharine Gun, and Clare Short.

53. These comments are available at http://www.madison.com/captimes/opinion/column/zweifel/6961.php.

54. See Carl Hulse and Philip Shenon, "Leaders of G.O.P. Try to Discredit a Critic of Bush," *New York Times,* March 27, 2004.

55. Philip Shenon and Elisabeth Bumiller, "Bush Allows Rice to Testify on 9/11 in a Public Session," *New York Times,* March 31, 2004.

56. Philip Shenon and David E. Sanger, "Bush Aides Kept Clinton's Papers from 9/11 Panel," *New York Times,* April 2, 2004.

57. Philip Shenon, "White House Agrees to Let Panel Review Clinton-Era Files," *New York Times,* April 3, 2004.

58. The article is by David Johnston and Eric Schmitt, *New York Times,* April 4, 2004. See also Douglas Jehl and David E. Sanger, "New to the Job, Rice Focused on More Traditional Threats," *New York Times,* April 5, 2004.

59. See David Johnston, "Top Bush Aide Is Questioned in C.I.A. Leak," *New York Times,* February 10, 2004; Richard W. Stevenson and David Johnston, "Anxiety Takes Hold of Presidential Aides Caught Up in Inquiry Over Leak," *New York Times,* February 12, 2004.

60. "Tracking Terrorist Bankrolls," *New York Times,* Editorial, April 4, 2004.

61. Lobe, "The Day Cheney Was Rocked to the Core," *Asia Times,* February 7, 2004.

62. "Pentagon Withholds Halliburton Payment," *New York Times,* March 18, 2004; Michael Janofsky, "Democrats Say Pentagon Questions Estimates on Iraq," *New York Times,* March 12, 2004.

63. "Iraq on the Record: The Bush Administration's Public Statement on Iraq," U.S. House of Representatives, Committee

on Government Reform, Minority Staff, Special Investigations Division, March 16, 2004, http://www.house.gov/reform/min/features/Iraq_on_the_record/.

64. Charles Tilly, *Coercion, Capital, and European States, AD 990–1990*, Basil Blackwell, p. 83. See also Charles Tilly, ed., *The Formation of National States in Western Europe*, Princeton University Press, 1975, especially the introductory essay by Charles Tilly, "Reflections on the History of European State-Making."

65. Dietrich Rueschemeyer, Evelyn Huber Stephens, and John D. Stephens, *Capitalist Development and Democracy*, University of Chicago Press, 1992, p. 70.

66. Göran Therborn, "The Rule of Capital and the Rise of Democracy," *New Left Review*.

67. Tilly, *Coercion, Capital, and European States, AD 990–1990*, Basil Blackwell, p. 31.

68. See Laura Jensen, *Patriots, Settlers, and the Origins of American Social Policy*, Cambridge University Press, 2003.

69. Quoted in William E. Leuchtenberg, "The Pertinence of Political History: Reflections on the Significance of the State in America," *Journal of American History* 73, no. 3 (1986), p. 592.

70. Eric Hobsbawm, "After the Winning of the War," *Le Monde Diplomatique*, June 2003.

CHAPTER 6

1. See several articles by Sam Dillion: "Bush Education Officials Find New Law a Tough Sell to States," *New York Times*, February 22, 2004; "President's Initiative to Shake Up Education Is Facing Protests in Many State Capitals, *New York*

Times, March 8, 2004; "U.S. Set to Ease Some Provisions of School Law," *New York Times,* March 14, 2004. See also Kate Zernike, "Attacks on Education Law Leave Democrats in a Bind," *New York Times,* January 12, 2004; and Diana Jean Schemo, "Rules Eased on Upgrading U.S. Schools," *New York Times,* March 16, 2004.

2. Diana Jean Schemo, "14 States Ask U.S. to Revise Some Education Law Rules," *New York Times,* March 25, 2004.

3. The 2005 Bush budget proposes to slice federal vocational and adult education funding by 35 percent, from $2.1 billion to $1.4 billion. See Jonathan Weisman, "What a $2.4 Trillion Budget Pays For," *Washington Post National Weekly Edition,* February 9–15, 2004.

4. Adam Nagourney with Richard W. Stevenson, "Pushing an Agenda, Far from Iraq," *New York Times,* April 5, 2004.

5. See Norman Ornstein, "Congress Inside Out," *Roll Call,* January 20, 2004; Ben Pershing and Erin P. Billings, "Ethics Moving on Smith Probe," *Roll Call,* February 5, 2004.

6. See Robert Pear, "U.S. Videos for TV News Come Under Scrutiny," *New York Times,* March 15, 2004; "The Actuary and the Actor," *New York Times,* Editorial, March 16, 2004.

7. Robert Pear and Edmund L. Andrews, "White House Says Congressional Estimate of New Medicare Costs Was Too Low," *New York Times,* February 2, 2004; Tony Pugh, "Bush Administration Ordered Medicare Plan Cost Estimates Withheld," *Knight Ridder Newspapers,* March 11, 2004; Robert Pear, "A Watchdog Sees Flaws in Bush's Ads on Medicare," *New York Times,* March 11, 2004; Lynette Clemetson, "Medicare Actuary Known for Strong Beliefs," *New York Times,* March 15, 2004; Sheryl Gay Stolberg and Robert Pear, "Mysterious Fax Adds to Intrigue Over Drug Bill," *New*

York Times, March 18, 2004; David Rogers, "Medicare's Chief Actuary Reveals E-Mail Warning," *Wall Street Journal,* March 18, 2004.

8. Robert Pear, "Inquiry Sought for Charge of Threat Over Medicare Data," *New York Times,* March 14, 2004; Robin Toner, "Seems the Last Word on Medicare Wasn't," *New York Times,* March 17, 2004; Robert Pear, "Medicare Official Testifies on Cost Figures," *New York Times,* March 25, 2004.

9. Robert Pear, "Medicare Overseers Expect Costs to Soar in Coming Decades," *New York Times,* March 24, 2004.

10. Robert Pear, "Senator Lott Says He Will Back Drug Imports," *New York Times,* March 12, 2004.

11. Rachel L. Swarns, "White House Irks Senators By Inaction on Immigrants," *New York Times,* March 24, 2004.

12. Shailagh Murray, "Arab-Americans Sour on Bush," *Wall Street Journal,* March 17, 2004.

13. Richard S. Dunham and Mike McNamee, with Howard Gleckman and Paul Magnusson, "Jobs: Desperately Seeking Answers," *BusinessWeek,* March 8, 2004.

14. Molly Ivins, "Wave Jobs Goodbye," *Alternet,* March 16, 2004.

15. Robert Pear and Richard W. Stevenson, "President Calls Economy Strong and Getting Stronger," *New York Times,* February 10, 2004.

16. Bob Herbert, "Promises, Promises," *New York Times*, February 16, 2004.

17. David Leonhardt, "Growth in Jobs Is Still Sluggish Despite Forecast," *New York Times,* March 6, 2004.

18. Richard W. Stevenson, "At Rally in Vital State, Bush Attacks Kerry on Economy," *New York Times,* March 21, 2004.

19. Moreover, features of the tax code (which are not attributable only to the Bush administration) actually reward companies for expanding overseas.

20. Eduardo Porter, "Data for March Show Big Surge in Job Creation," *New York Times,* April 3, 2004.

21. Laura D'Andrea Tyson, "The Recovery Could Be Built on Quicksand," *BusinessWeek,* March 29, 2004.

22. Todd Buchholz, "Only Machines Need Apply," *New York Times,* March 19, 2004.

23. See Louis Uchitelle, "Growth in Jobs Ground to Halt During December, *New York Times,* January 10, 2004, and Uchitelle, "To Understand U.S. Jobs Picture, Connect the Dots, and Find the Dots," *New York Times,* January 12, 2004, and "New Patterns Restrict Hiring," *New York Times,* March 6, 2004; David Leonhardt, "Even for Financial Experts, Analyzing the Job Market is an Adventure," *New York Times, Business Day,* January 12, 2004; Jared Bernstein and Lawrence Mishel, "Labor Market Left Behind," *Economic Policy Institute Briefing Paper,* 2004. And see various reports on "Jobs Picture" at the Economic Policy Institute website: http://jobwatfh.org/index.html.

24. See Doug Henwood, "The New Economy and After," *Left Business Observer,* January 24, 2004, p. 106; David M. Gordon, *Fat and Mean: The Corporate Squeeze of Working Americans and the Myth of Managerial "Downsizing,"* Free Press, 1996; William J. Baumol, Alan S. Blinder, and Edward N. Wolff, *Downsizing in America: Reality, Causes, and Consequences,* Russell Sage Foundation, 2004.

25. See James K. Galbraith, "Works on Progress," *American Prospect,* January 2004.

26. See Robert L. Borosage, "The Kitchen-Table State of the Union," *Nation,* February 2, 2004. According to the industry

consulting firm Gartner Inc. one in ten U.S. technology jobs will move overseas by the end of 2004, and over the next fifteen years some 3.3 million U.S. service-sector jobs will be sent abroad, according to a November 2002 study by the consulting firm Forrester Research. See Kevin Danaher and Jason Mark, "White Collar Anger," *Alternet,* December 18, 2003.

27. Richard S. Dunham, ed., "Outsource This: The Dems Smell Blood," *BusinessWeek,* March 1, 2004.

28. See Harold Meyerson, "Plutocrats and Populists," *Washington Post,* February 5, 2004.

29. See Sarah Anderson and John Cavanagh, Jeff Madrick, and Doug Henwood in the feature "Toward a Progressive View on Outsourcing," *Nation,* March 22, 2004.

30. See Bruce Nussbaum, "Special Report: Economic Growth Is Very Strong, But America Isn't Generating Enough Jobs. Many Blame Outsourcing. The Truth Is Alot More Complicated," *BusinessWeek,* March 22, 2004.

31. Bob Herbert, "Trouble in Bush's America," *New York Times,* May 8, 2003.

32. Molly Ivins, "Wave Jobs Goodbye," *Alternet,* March 16, 2004.

33. See Laura D'Andrea Tyson, "This Recovery Could Be Built on Quicksand," *BusinessWeek,* March 29, 2004.

34. See Robert Greenstein and Isaac Shapiro, "The New, Definitive CBO Data on Income and Tax Trends," Center on Budget and Policy Priorities, September 23, 2003.

35. Bob Herbert, "We're More Productive: Who Gets the Money?" *New York Times,* April 5, 2004. Herbert is reporting on a study by Andrew Sum et al., "The Unprecedented Rising Tide of Corporate Profits and the Simultaneous Ebbing of Labor Compensation—Gainers and Losers from the Na-

tional Economic Recovery in 2002 and 2003," Center for Labor Market Studies, Northeastern University, 2004.

36. Louis Uchitelle, "This Economic Recovery Is Unkind to Workers," *New York Times,* December 21, 2003.

37. Patrick McGeehan, "Again, Money Follows the Pinstripes," *New York Times,* Money and Business section, April 6, 2003. "Key Facts on CEO Pay," *Executive PayWatch,* AFL-CIO, April 15, 2003. In 2003, executive pay appeared to shrink, but all of the decline came from a drop in the amount of options granted them last year, and so was purely theoretical. Cash earnings actually increased sharply in 2003. See Patrick McGeehan, "Is C.E.O. Pay Up or Down? Both," *New York Times,* Money and Business Section, April 4, 2003. http://www.unionvoice.org/campaign/ceopaytaxcuts/xkxgayj7wx.

38. See William Branigin, "U.S. Consumer Debt Grows at Alarming Rate," *Washington Post,* January 12, 2004; Louis Uchitelle, "Hey, Big Spender, the U.S. Economic Recovery Needs You," *International Herald Tribune,* December 1, 2003; OMB Watch, "Economy and Jobs Watch: Consumer Debt Increases, Savings Rate Down," http://www.omb watch.org/article/view/1938/1/2.

39. Katrina vanden Heuvel, "What Economic Recovery?" November 25, 2003, http://www.thenation.com/edcut/index mhtml?bid=78&pic=1093.

40. Mary Leonard, "Homelessness, Hunger Worsen, Mayors' Report Finds," *Boston Globe,* December 20, 2003.

41. Harold Meyerson, "Democrats Break a Taboo," *Washington Post,* February 28, 2004.

42. James K. Galbraith, "Why Bush *Likes* a Bad Economy," *Progressive,* October 2003.

43. Sarah Ferguson, "Thousands March for Peace," *Alternet,* March 22, 2004.

44. Andrew Gumbel, "How the War Machine Is Driving the U.S. Economy: Military Keynesianism Might Get Bush Re-elected, But It Is Starting to Worry Economists," *Independent/UK,* January 6, 2004.

45. Galbraith, "Why Bush *Likes* a Bad Economy," *Progressive,* October 2003.

46. Edmund L. Andrews and Robert Pear, "Entitlement Costs Are Expected to Soar," *New York Times,* March 19, 2004.

47. Robert J. Barro, "It's the Spending Stupid—Not the Deficit," *BusinessWeek,* March 1, 2004.

48. "Conservatives Simmer as US Spending Mushrooms Under Bush," Dow Jones Newswires, *Wall Street Journal,* January 5, 2004.

49. See Robert Pear and Edmund L. Andrews, "Bush to Back Off Some Initiatives for Budget Plan," *New York Times,* February 1, 2004; Carl Hulse, "House G.O.P. Leaders, Under Pressure, Weight Cutting Bush's Budget," *New York Times,* February 12, 2004.

50. Richard Oppel Jr. "Bush Plans for Tax Cuts Barely Avert House Setback," *New York Times,* March 31, 2004; also by Oppel, "House Republicans Defeat an Effort to Limit Tax Cuts," *New York Times,* March 26, 2004; "Flogging the House Rules," *New York Times,* Editorial, March 31, 2004.

51. Richard Oppel Jr. "Senate Approves Budget Intended to Curb Deficit," *New York Times,* March 13, 2004.

52. Elisabeth Bumiller, "Bush Acts to Ease the Furor Over Jobs Shipped Abroad," *New York Times,* February 13, 2004.

53. Neil A. Lewis, "President Makes His Pitch on Jobs and at Ballgame," *New York Times,* April 6, 2004.

54. Elizabeth Becker, "Globalism Minus Jobs Equals Campaign Issue," *New York Times,* January 30, 2004.

55. Sheila Crowley, "Point of View," memo to members, weekly newsletter of the National Low Income Housing Coalition, March 26, 2004.

56. Horn is quoted in Robert Pear, "Despite Sluggish Economy, Welfare Rolls Actually Shrank," *New York Times,* March 22, 2004. On welfare reform and recession, see Barbara Ehrenreich and Frances Fox Piven, "Without a Safety Net," *Mother Jones,* May–June 2002.

57. Robert Pear, "Defying Bush, Senate Increases Child Care Funds for the Poor," *New York Times,* March 31, 2004.

58. Robert Pear, "Senate, Torn by Minimum Wage, Shelves Major Welfare Bill," *New York Times,* April 2, 2004; "TANF Update," Center for Community Change Policy Alert #320, March 31, 2004.

59. *Hardship in Many Languages: Immigrant Families and Children in NYC,* Milano Graduate School, Center for New York City Affairs, New School University, January 2004.

60. Adrienne Lu, "Agencies Say Hunger on Rise Outside Cities Across Region," *New York Times,* March 23, 2004.

61. "The State of the Union: In Search of a Theme," *Economist,* January 24, 2004.

62. Martha A. Sandweiss, "Death on the Front Page," *New York Times,* April 4, 2004.

63. Quoted in Danny Schechter, "Clarke and the Media Failures of 9/11," *MediaChannel.org,* March 30, 2004, http://www/mediachannel.org/views/dissector/affalert165.shtml.

64. Stan Crock et al., "That's One Problem Solved," *BusinessWeek,* December 29, 2003.

65. The trial of Saddam could, however, backfire if he and his

lawyers succeed in revealing the role of the United States as long-term allies of his regime, until the Gulf War.

66. Carl Hulse, "Senate Outlaws Injury to Fetus During a Crime," *New York Times,* March 26, 2004; "Reproductive Rights Assaulted," *New York Times,* Editorial, April 5, 2004.

67. See Susan Saulney, "Foes of Federal Ban on Abortion Method Are to Argue Their Cases in Courts in Three States," *New York Times,* March 29, 2004; Michael Ventura, "Protecting Your Privates," *Austin Chronicle,* March 24, 2004. Attorney General Ashcroft says he needs the records to help him defend the law prohibiting partial-birth abortions.

68. "Down and Dirty in the Gun Debate," *New York Times,* February 27, 2004.

69. Cited by Paul Krugman, "This Isn't America," *New York Times,* March 30, 2004.

70. Rupert Cornwall, writing in the *Independent,* and cited in "Fathers and Sons (Part 2)," Tomeditor@aol.com, March 24, 2004.

71. See Larry Hugick and Alec M. Gallup, "'Rally Events' and Presidential Approval," paper presented at the annual meeting of the American Association for Public Opinion Research in Phoenix, May 1991.